W9-AXH-148

Hoover Institution Publications 137

The Struggle for Cyprus

DS54.8
F583

The Struggle for Cyprus

Charles Foley

and

W. I. Scobic

MAY 0 6 1975

Hoover Institution Press
Stanford University
Stanford, California

187411

The Hoover Institution on War, Revolution and Peace, founded at Stanford University in 1919 by the late President Herbert Hoover, is a center for advanced study and research on public and international affairs in the twentieth century. The views expressed in its publications are entirely those of the authors and do not necessarily reflect the views of the staff, officers, or Board of Overseers of the Hoover Institution.

Library of Congress Cataloging in Publication Data

Foley, Charles, 1908–
    The struggle for Cyprus.

    (Hoover Institution publications, 137)
    Bibliography: p.
    1. Cyprus—History.   I. Scobie, W. I., 1932–
joint author.   II. Title.   III. Series: Stanford
University. Hoover Institution on War, Revolution, and
Peace. Publications, 137.
DS54.8.F583   956.4′503   74-10837
ISBN 0-8179-1371-8

Hoover Institution Publications 137
International Standard Book Number 0–8179–1371–8
Library of Congress Catalog Card Number 74-10837
© 1975 by the Board of Trustees of the
        Leland Stanford Junior University
All rights reserved
Printed in the United States of America

To our friends and colleagues of the *Times of Cyprus*, a newspaper with ideas of its own, we gratefully dedicate this footnote to our labors.

Archbishop Makarios III

General George Grivas

Contents

Preface

During the 1955–1960 revolution in Cyprus, the authors of this book worked on the *Times of Cyprus,* an English-language newpaper which tried to hold a balance between contending factions, and found themselves in daily contact with events and with many of the leading personalities concerned. During the Republic's lifespan, 1960-1974, they attempted to separate fact from propaganda and establish the motivation behind developments that at the time had been obscured by censorship or distorted by hearsay. The resulting monograph depended for its sources on a multitude of witnesses and a considerable body of documentation on Cypriot guerrilla operations and British counterinsurgency measures.

The scope of the inquiry extended to the international level, for the troubles in Cyprus, which achieved its independence in 1960 after eighty-two years of British rule, had threatened the political balance of the Mediterranean, brought Greece and Turkey to the brink of war, and taxed U.S. diplomacy in preserving NATO's Eastern defenses. Among the figures interviewed in Athens, Ankara, New York, London, and Cyprus during and after the conflict were Harold Macmillan, former prime minister of Britain; the late Adnan Menderes and Ismet Inonu, two premiers of Turkey; George Stratos and Evangelos Averoff, two former foreign ministers of Greece; Field-Marshal Harding and Sir Hugh Foot, the last two governors of Cyprus. Archbishop Makarios, who held the reins of policy during the struggle and who has been the Republic's president every since, talked with great candor and detail of the revolt he had inspired. General George Grivas, field commander of the revolt, submitted to exhaustive questioning in Athens, Zurich, and Cyprus. He also released his followers from the oath of silence they had taken concerning their activities in EOKA (National Organization of Cypriot Fighters), so that each might contribute what he knew of the events. More than three hundred persons within that secret organization were interviewed, and their accounts cross-checked both with quantities of documentary evidence—EOKA orders and correspondence, British security files, contemporary newspaper and other reports—and with the evidence given by EOKA's political and military leaders.

While it would be impractical to name everyone who helped us over the years from 1955 to 1972, we should like to mention at least a few of them here. Chief among these are Archbishop Makarios and General Grivas, who with courtesy and patience gave so many hours of their time. We were also generously assisted by the late Polycarpos Georgadjis, minister of the interior, and numerous other EOKA members now in the Cyprus government or Parliament, among them Andreas Azinas, Tassos Papadopolous, Nicos Koshis, Nicos Sampson, and the three sisters who ran EOKA's distaff side, Loulla, Ourania, and Maroulla Kokkinou. Socrates Eliades, formerly General Grivas' right-hand man in Cyprus, drove us over the island to introduce EOKA figures. Grivas' old friend and lawyer Christos Papadopolous, and the general's brother, Dr. Michael Grivas, enlightened us on the general's early days. Prof. Andreas Papandreou, a member of the Greek cabinet from 1964 to 1965, contributed special insights into the role of Athens in Cypriot politics.

Our greatest debt, however, is to four old friends who were always ready with advice and assistance: Glafkos Clerides, deputy-president of the Republic and formerly legal adviser to the *Times of Cyprus;* Leslie Finer, author and correspondent for the London *Observer* and the *Times of Cyprus;* and Dr. Vassos Lysarides and his wife Barbara, also an author and *Times of Cyprus* correspondent, who introduced us to many of the people in this book and were a mine of knowledge concerning the intricate workings of Cypriot politics. Finally, our deepest gratitude goes to Miss Christine Tapley for the time, energy, and devotion she gave to putting the manuscript into shape for publication.

February, 1974   C. F.

                                                                     W. S.

Introduction

A history of bondage that goes back to the beginnings of recorded time [1] came to a close with the revolution of 1955–1960 through which the Cypriot people withdrew from an empire in decline to declare an independent republic. The island is not large, but it has always had strategic importance and the British were only the latest in a long line of occupiers—Phoenicians, Greeks, Romans, Byzantines, Crusaders, Lusignans, Venetians, Turks—to take it as a base for naval and military purposes. The new Republic's life was brief: in 1974, after its president had been overthrown by a military coup, an invading Turkish army once more occupied a large part of the island.

Cyprus had been for three hundred years a neglected outpost of the Ottoman Empire when Disraeli conceived the idea of acquiring it from Turkey, the "sick man of Europe." He offered some reasons for doing so in a characteristically highflown letter dated May 5, 1878:

> If Cyprus be conceded to Your Majesty by the Porte, and England, at the same time, enters into a Defensive Alliance with Turkey, guaranteeing Asiatic Turkey from Russian invasion, the power of England in the Mediterranean will be absolutely increased in that region, and Your Majesty's Indian Empire immensely strengthened. Cyprus is the key to Western Asia. [2]

It was, in fact, nothing of the sort, though its occupation helped to bolt a back door to Britain's overseas possessions. Disraeli's object was to keep Russia from the Mediterranean and so out of reach of Turkey, the Middle East, and the sea routes to India. The Cypriot population

1

was not, at this or any previous change of ownership, consulted about its wishes. One month after his letter to the queen, Disraeli won Turkish agreement to the British occupation of Cyprus in return for a pledge to guarantee the Sultan's Asiatic possessions against Russia.

On July 12, 1878, the Union Jack was raised in Nicosia, the capital of the island, as the last Turkish governor handed possession over to the British. Lieutenant-General Sir Garnet Wolseley (later field marshal) landed with British and Indian troops. In a welcoming address, the bishop of Kitium, spiritual and—in the absence of Cypriot political in-stitutions—temporal leader of the Greek-speaking majority, seized the opportunity to tell Sir Garnet: ''We accept the change of Government inasmuch as we trust that Great Britain will help Cyprus, as she did the Ionian islands, to be united with Mother Greece, with which it is natu-rally connected.'' It was the first of a myriad such protestations that would fall on unheeding British ears.

A local grain merchant who was to become the father of George Grivas, future field leader of the uprising, was among those who watched the first British troops run up a flag that was to become familiar on government offices, if nowhere else.

The new occupiers were honest, dutiful, and unimaginative. They built roads, replanted forests, and eliminated the ancient scourge of ma-laria which had sapped the energy of the people. They saw to it that the Greek Cypriots who composed four-fifths of the population lived in peace with the remainder, who were Turks; the practice of religion, whether Greek Orthodox or Moslem, and educational loyalties to Greece or Turkey were undisturbed as part of the tradition of colonial rule in letting well enough alone.

After three centuries of Turkish oppression, the Greek Cypriots looked with hope and patience to British ideals of freedom which would surely meet their aspirations toward union with Greece in course of time. They rejoiced when Gladstone, Disraeli's rival, who had con-demned the acquisition of Cyprus, later publicly advocated its transfer to Greece; but when he returned to office he did nothing to achieve that end.

From then on, for three-quarters of a century, the path to Union seemed, in Greek eyes, to be strewn with broken promises. At first the British could say that the island was not theirs to give since legally it was on lease from Turkey. Then, during World War I, when the Turks entered the conflict on the German side, Cyprus was annexed by Britain and offered in 1915 to Greece as an inducement to join the Allies. Athens was not prepared at that time to enter the war, and when she agreed to do so the British said that the decision had come too late.

In 1925 the British declared the island a crown colony and from that point on, for thirty years, refused to consider any prospect of its eventual union with Greece.

For their part, the Cypriots issued manifestoes to succeeding governors and organized demonstrations and riots and even a minor uprising in 1931 to persuade the rulers that the Greek Cypriots persisted in their wish for union with Greece. A Cypriot mob burned down Government House. But the only result of these activities was that the Cypriots lost such constitutional liberties as they possessed, and were obliged to pay for the construction of the splendid residence that has become today's Presidential Palace. The bishops of Kitium and Kyrenia, considered guilty of inciting the riot, were exiled, and British officials increasingly held the view that "Enosis" (union with Greece) was "a Frankenstein's monster" created by the Church, which forced Cypriots to pay lip service "when all that most of them have wanted is to be left alone." [3]

Of several aspects of Cyprus which baffled the administrators, none seemed so strange or so antipathetic, as the Orthodox Church. They did not appreciate its esoteric form of Christianity; and they abhorred its pretensions to the political leadership of the Cypriot people, a role thrust upon it by a series of invaders through centuries of foreign rule. This attitude had persisted during much of the island's history, and in earlier days had resulted in persecution of the bishops. In 1821, following the outbreak of the Greek War of Independence, when unrest in Cyprus was feared, the Turkish governor Kuchuk Mehmed, had seized Kyprianos, the archbishop of Cyprus, and the three bishops of Paphos, Kitium, and Kyrenia together with all notable ecclesiastics and laymen. After humiliations and tortures, these dignitaries were hanged, beheaded, or otherwise dispatched by way of a warning to potential rebels.

Such methods were alien to the British who in 1878 had succeeded the Turks; they were often dedicated and scholarly men—none more so than the governor, Sir Ronald Storrs, who arrived in 1926 and whose lot it was to decide the fate of the "instigators" of the 1931 uprising. Sir Ronald, soldier, author, and civil servant, aide to Lord Kitchener and friend to Lawrence of Arabia, found the island he had been appointed to govern in lamentable condition, "financially spoiled, politically spoilt." A "legislative council" existed on which Greeks sat, but though "the real interests of the Colony were those of the peasant producer'' the interests represented in the legislature were those of "the parasites who made a living out of him." [4]

Storrs also found the cause of the keenest of Cypriot economic grievances against the British. Under the 1878 convention, a tribute that would be raised by taxation in Cyprus had been promised to the Sultan. And raised it was, but year after year the money went to London, where it was used to pay off Turkey's debts to the Ottoman government bondholders. Sir Ronald persuaded Whitehall to abolish the tribute, at least in name. Instead, the Cypriots were required to make a contribution toward the cost of imperial defense, a sum which—coincidentally—equalled the gap between British grants to the island and the tribute extracted from it. This practice toward a poor and backward island was a major cause of the unrest that culminated in the 1931 uprising, which the British suppressed with the arrest of two thousand people, the wounding of thirty and the killing of six. There were no government casualties.

In considering the discontent of the Cypriots under British rule, however, one is led to feel that economic shortcomings were a lesser cause for complaint than were the administrators' social and racial prejudices. The Cypriots could only deduce from the circumstances that these servants of the government were in Cyprus to administer justice and keep the peace, not to please the governed. Most of the administrators had had experience only in backward territories where the native was kept firmly in his place; and in this very different land with its rich culture and long traditions, they maintained their condescending stance. Most officials came into social contact mainly with a handful of wealthy Cypriots who were admitted to the larger functions, such as the garden party held to celebrate the Queen's official birthday. Even these too often found their customs patronized and their ambitions thwarted: despite their evident abilities Cypriots in every profession and walk of life, excepting the Church, were limited in advancement.

The Cypriots continued to live for the two decades following Sir Ronald's departure in 1932 with the form of authoritarian government he bequeathed. Then, in 1948, a Labour government in Britain offered a new constitution which would have increased Cypriot representation in the Legislative Council. The Cypriot leaders rejected it, declaring that they wanted only Enosis. The government replied by passing a sedition law which banned Enosis in speech and print. Nor need the Cypriots ever hope to obtain union with Greece, as they were warned by a minister of state for colonial affairs in the succeeding Conservative government. British Middle East Headquarters, forced out of Suez by Egypt's President Nasser in July, 1954, was to be permanently relocated in Cyprus.

The difficulties of attempting to convince a people who had since time immemorial clung to Greek thought, faith, and language that they were not in fact Greek did not deter the British from the endeavor. And when arguments proved unavailing, a gallimaufry of illiberal edicts was introduced by successive governors, all aimed at the suppression of the Enosis movement. Laws restricted the ringing of church bells and the flying of Greek flags. The governor might suspend publication of any newspaper without the right of appeal to a court of law. Sir Herbert Richmond Palmer, who arrived as governor from West Africa in 1934, earned a place in Cyprus history when he barred any person from becoming archbishop without his personal approval. An outraged Church refused to elect a prelate to the throne which had become vacant, but Sir Herbert's edict was not repealed for eleven years, until the second World War had run its course.

There can have been few Cypriots who did not feel from day to day the bitterness of submission to foreign rule. While in most colonies government was passing to the people, in Cyprus paternalism had become more autocratic in this century than the last.

Such feelings were certainly a motivating force in the character of George Grivas, who was born on May 23, 1898, in the village of Trikomo, near Famagusta. It is difficult to appreciate at this distance in time the insistence and strength of the forces that molded his generation. From his mother he heard the tales and songs of Dighenis Akritas, the legendary folk hero of Byzantine Cyprus; he saw the craggy rock once hurled in anger by this local Herakles into the Greek sea. Grivas' father was a well-to-do corn broker, owner of the largest house in a village that was the center of a thriving agricultural community. The family worshipped in the twelfth-century Church of the Blessed Virgin Mary among peasants whose faces were mirrored in the medieval paintings on the walls, a people whose faith had been preserved through ten centuries of foreign domination.

The young Grivas relished the open-air life. His passion, as a boy, was to gallop along the white sands of Famagusta bay, to the alarm of his more stolid elder brother Michael. A half-hour's ride down the coast lay the ruins of Salamis, a Greek city half buried in the sands, where he might muse on the patriot-king Evagoras, who had secured the island's freedom from the Persians in the fifth century B.C.; or on the Mycenean colony that had existed there before the Trojan War.

The idea of reviving the Greek world to freedom and power was central to his upbringing. At home and in school George Grivas was surrounded by portraits of the men of 1821—the year when the Greek War of Independence broke out: Prince Alexander Ypsilanti, leader of the secret "liberation committees" that plotted the overthrow of the Turks; Archbishop Germanos, who unfurled the standard of Greece and led forty thousand peasants against the tyrant; and many more. Grivas' special hero was Karaiskakis, an early master of guerrilla warfare, whose skills recovered most of continental Greece, although much of it was lost again at his death. Grivas saw the 1821–1830 conflict as basically a guerrilla struggle.[5] Bands of irregulars cohered eventually into an army, aided by foreign Philhellenes, but still it employed guerrilla methods against the vastly superior forces of the Ottoman Empire.

In 1908, Grivas' last year at the village school, the island of Crete proclaimed union with Greece in the name of King George of the Hellenes; but to the incredulity of the Grivas household and many another in the Greek world, the Athens government hesitated to sanction union, fearing Turkish reaction. This betrayal of the cause, as many saw it, resulted in the revolt of the Military League, a band of young army officers, and led the way to the open intervention of the Army in Greek politics which persists to this day.

George Grivas had already decided on a military career. In 1916 he gained entrance to the Athenian military academy known as "The School of the Promising Ones" and graduated among the first rank of cadets. He was placed at once on active service in Turkey, where the Greek army was trying to secure territories around Smyrna.

Grivas here had his first taste of guerrilla warfare, as his division mopped up Turkish irregulars in the mountains around Smyrna. He was struck by the enemy's determination and success: small bands of riflemen were able to hold off an entire division for a full day until artillery was brought up against them. The Greek army advanced to within sixty miles of Ankara when it was thrown back by the Turks. The reversal was complete: the Greeks were ousted from Asia Minor and a fearful massacre of Christians took place in the sack of Smyrna.

A long spell in military limbo followed. Grivas was gazetted a captain at the age of twenty-six and was sent to France for studies at army schools. As a lieutenant-colonel on the general staff when World War II broke out, he saw active service against Mussolini's invading forces on the northern front, and when the German armies overran Greece he evaded capture and returned to Athens.

There, in 1943, he organized a "private army" which eventually numbered some three hundred men, mostly officers of royalist sympathies. He called it "X" (a letter of the Greek alphabet and a symbol for the unknown). Its purpose was not only to oppose the powerful Communist guerrilla forces then roaming the Greek countryside but also to resist the Germans, against whom "X's" activities were limited largely to intelligence work and propaganda for the British in the Middle East. Grivas blamed this limitation and consequent inaction of the nationalist guerrillas on Churchill's policy of arming and supporting the more numerous and better organized leftist groups, such as ELAS [6] which had an army numbering forty thousand.

When in December 1944 the Greek Communists tried to seize control of the country, "X" took an active part in street fighting against ELAS. The Communists were driven from Athens but in the succeeding civil war more than twenty thousand people died and Greece was economically ruined. Grivas held the British responsible in large measure for the tragedy by their wartime policy of abetting the Communist forces; he wrote in his memoirs:

> I had, up to that moment, always been wholeheartedly pro-British; but in the years that followed I found it hard to forget the frivolous role played by the rulers of Britain. [7]

Grivas next attempted to turn "X" into a political party for the first postwar elections. But his extreme right-wing views, and also perhaps his irascible rigidity repelled all but a tiny portion of the electorate.

This political activity, however, did result in an encounter that was to be of lasting significance for Cyprus. Shortly after World War II, in 1946, Grivas was introduced by Zaphyrios Valvis, his aide in "X", to Michael Mouskos, the young priest of the fashionable Athenian Church of St. Irene. Grivas was by now a well-known figure in Athenian politics. Michael Mouskos was an obscure priest sent from his monastery in Cyprus to study theology at Athens University, and only recently ordained. But the obscure priest was to become one of the outstanding figures in history; for this was the future Archbishop Makarios, one of the heroes of the Cypriot revolution.

One sees the two of them: the peppery little colonel with the wiry body and the fiercely waxed moustache; and the bright young priest, son of a shepherd, who had risen from the ranks of the novitiate and was clearly destined for high ecclesiastical office. When they met, Grivas was almost fifty years of age, married but childless, a man without hope of advancement who yet remained ambitious. Michael Mouskos was nearly twenty years younger, but remarkably assured: tall and elegant in his black soutane. He came from Panayia, a village in the Troodos foothills where as a boy he had often tended the flocks. He had spent months at a time living with his father in a shed beside the sheepfold, before beginning his education at Kykko monastery, one of the wealthier and more powerful institutions of the Orthodox Church. He had lived out the war years in Athens.

The youthful priest sensed Grivas' extremism, but believed that he might render services to the Cyprus cause. In 1946, he offered some articles for the "X" news sheet, and they were accepted. In them Mouskos pleased Grivas by attacking Communism "from a Christian viewpoint." [8]

A few months later, in September of that year, the young priest sailed for the United States, where he was to study at Boston University College. Before his studies were completed, however, he had been elected bishop of Kitium by the Church dignitaries who had sent him to the United States. He returned to take up his duties and in 1949, on one of his first missions to sound out the strength of support for Enosis in Athens, he again met Grivas. They talked only in generalities, but the meeting was decisive: for the new bishop was already thinking of "doing something against the British," [9] and he was much impressed by Grivas' strong personality and will. He was given, too, an example of the Grivas' stubborn single-mindedness, as he related later:

> When the General Election took place in Athens after the war, I advised Grivas not to divide the national forces but to join with the Popular Party of Tsaldaris, who offered 20 seats. Grivas was annoyed and went ahead alone. He did not win a single seat. [10]

In 1950, at the age of thirty-seven, Michael Mouskos was elected to the supreme post of Archbishop of Cyprus and took the name Makarios III. By tradition he became also ethnarch, or civil leader of the Greek

Cypriots, the title deriving from the days of the Ottoman Empire when the archbishop was recognized as petitioner for his community before the Sultan's throne.

Makarios now concentrated his efforts to attain Enosis, by going over the heads of the British occupiers by publicizing the question of Cyprus abroad,

> . . . for if we decided to use force it would have no effect, or little, since people even in Greece knew next to nothing of the problem. I tried to create an issue, as Bishop and Archbishop, by making speeches at monasteries in the mountains, by visits to foreign countries and publicity generally. But I was still criticized in the press, which said publicity was not enough.[11]

Makarios' major coup was the organization by the Church of a plebiscite in Cyprus, in which ninety-eight percent of the population was reported to have voted for Enosis. The response of the British administrators was that the people had voted as they had, only because they had been threatened with excommunication and other spiritual sanctions, and that the plebiscite was in any case meaningless. But they had begun to recognize that here was a man who, in Sir Anthony Eden's words, "was out to make as much difficulty as possible," and would further infect the Cypriots with "the universal bacillus of nationalism." It was the opinion of Sir Anthony, who was to become Britain's prime minister in the very month that the revolt began in Cyprus, that colony after colony was attempting to run before it could walk; and he saw no pressing reason why Cyprus should do either.[12]

However, if there was indeed a sizable portion of the population that did not support the new archbishop in his agitation for Enosis, it was not easy to discover. The two or three wealthy and educated Cypriots who had been admitted to the governor's councils might deprecate to His Excellency's face the new activism, but behind his back, among their fellow Greeks, they usually sang a different tune. Even the local Marxists of AKEL (Cypriot Progressive Workers Party) who had pretensions to being the socialist opposition to the Church, urged not merely an end to "imperialism," but also union with Greece. The contradiction of a Communist party that desired Enosis with a country ruled by a monarchy branded elsewhere as "fascist" was carried over into AKEL's public demonstrations, where no hint of red was seen. The marching comrades carried Greek flags with crosses on the top of poles; their organizers wore blue and white armbands. Although some of its leaders had been trained in the Soviet Union, the real strength of the left resided in the trade unions, which were solidly behind the demand for Enosis.

Five months after mounting the archiepiscopal throne, Makarios III paid his first visit as ethnarch to the Greek capital. It was March 13, 1951: the Korean war dragged on; in America, all eyes were fixed on the conflict between President Truman and General MacArthur; and the British were occupied with the "emergencies" in Malaya and Kenya, and the prospect later that year of their first Conservative government since the end of World War II. There was little interest in the activities of the Archbishop of Cyprus.

He found in Athens several groups dedicated to the liberation of the island, or at least to vehement discussion of its necessity. One such body presented itself to him at a reception in the Grand Bretagne, the main hotel, where its leader made a speech publicly declaring his readiness to fight the British. A large audience applauded. Makarios thanked him, and thought that, if nothing else, it was an index of public feeling. He looked more seriously on a committee headed by two Cypriot brothers, Savvas and Socrates Loizides, who were also lawyers, and included no less a figure than the popular George Stratos, former minister of war and a personal friend of King George of Greece. Makarios attended one of the committee's meetings. Stratos was an influential figurehead; but if force should ever be used in Cyprus they needed the right kind of military mind. The Archbishop suggested Grivas, the leader of "X", whom he had met some eighteen months before. And in April, after doing his utmost to make the Greek government raise the Cyprus question at the United Nations, he asked Socrates Loizides to bring Colonel Grivas into their liberation committee.

The brothers invited Grivas to the Tsitsas Cafe, one of those spacious Athenian establishments dedicated to the discussion of politics over innumerable small cups of strong black coffee. It stands among the series of neo-classical buildings that line University Street, under the eye of a marble statue of Gladstone, British liberator of the Ionian isles. At a corner table in a secluded part of the balcony the conspirators met.

Savvas Loizides, the older brother, was soft-spoken and slow, Socrates excitable and impulsive. Savvas was the diplomat: as head of the Cyprus ethnarchy office in Athens it was his task to attempt to make a dent in the world's indifference toward his homeland's plight, and he had for years endured the apathy of editors and politicians from Paris to

New York. Socrates, who had seen some action against the Communists, and had been exiled from Cyprus as a dangerous agitator, was eager for fresh adventure.

Savvas explained to Grivas their committee's purposes and asked him if he was willing to organize and lead a band of guerrillas in Cyprus. Socrates said that he knew from personal experience in the island that the young people would follow him to a man.

Grivas had long entertained thoughts of leading a revolt in Cyprus. He had revealed them to a few intimate friends, such as his old colonel from the 30th Infantry, General G. Kosmas—now chief of the general staff, who had the ear of the prime minister, Field Marshal Papagos; but without result. Now he accepted the offer with a reply that was as long as it was passionate, carrying the others away on the flood of rhetoric. An hour later the meeting broke up in a glow of patriotic sentiment. It was agreed that Grivas should make a personal tour of Cyprus to refresh his mind on possibilities for sabotage and guerrilla warfare.

Grivas sailed for Cyprus on July 5, 1951, taking his wife Kiki, to give a holiday air to his reconnaissance of the island which was his birthplace.

— 1 —

Rumblings of Revolution

The country that Archbishop Makarios and Colonel Grivas set out in 1951 to wrest from British control is far from ideal for planners of a guerrilla war. Its small size (3,584 square miles), its isolation and distance from potential sources of supply in Greece, the ease with which it could be blockaded by the British Navy—all these were unfavorable. The terrain, too, seems at first sight hostile: Nicosia, the capital, is an ancient walled city. It lies in the great central plain which the summer heat turns to a shimmering desert that offers no refuge beyond some scattered villages. Yet five thousand feet up in the Troodos mountains, fires and blankets are a necessity; in winter the snow makes roads impassable. The British had built many roads that would allow the rapid transfer of troops to the scene of an attack or to points where they might sever rebel supply lines. The Kyrenia range of mountains, which runs along the north coast, was even less suitable than was the Troodos range for Grivas' purpose. Its narrow line of peaks, sweeping upward from the coastal meadows in a series of crags and precipices, is crowned with three summits on which stand the remains of castles built by Latin knights and kings. Ruined keeps and bastions look out across the Mediterranean to the far-off mountains of southern Turkey; and though they no doubt served their Frankish builders well in medieval times, they symbolized precisely what Grivas intended to avoid in his campaign: isolated strongholds that offered themselves to attack. His aim was the creation of an invisible army that would cover the whole island, living in the villages and towns—present everywhere but showing itself nowhere.

These urban guerrillas, he recognized, could not survive without the support of the population, because it was to the people that the revolutionaries must constantly turn for hiding places, food supplies, couriers, propaganda, and new recruits. Here was the rub; the island's five hundred twenty-four thousand Greek Cypriots [1] were by nature placid; they had resisted passively under successive conquests, but they had never resorted to arms. The British believed they never would, and said so. When Richard Crossman, M.P., visited Cyprus in 1954, one year before hostilities began, officials of the island told him that if the Cypriot people really wanted Enosis they would fight for it. This view was communicated to the Archbishop, who thought it "rather provocative."

Grivas believed the people could be organized and the bravest youth trained as guerrillas; it was his opinion that the Cypriot temperament "could be fanned into flame by one strong breath"; [2] but he did not foresee the extent to which the draconian measures adopted by the British would assist him by estranging the Greek population from the government and incline the people to his side. Nor, on the other hand, did he gauge the manner in which the rulers would employ the Turkish minority of some ninety-two thousand as a political lever and militant body against him.

Throughout the summer months of 1951, Grivas toured the island, paying particular attention to the Troodos mountain area and its two most hospitable valleys, the Solea and the Marathassa, which run between grey peaks, watered by perennial streams, and filled with poplars and fruit trees on the lower slopes. From a house rented in Kalapanayotis by his brother Michael, a prominent Nicosia physician, he made forays into the pine forests westward toward the isolated monastery of Kykko. Villages are few in these wild forest stretches and he hoped that the monastery would act as a supply center for guerrilla bands. In a village famous for its sulphur baths he met Bishop Kyprianos of Kyrenia, who had come to take the waters. People generally, he found, were skeptical about the chances of an armed uprising, recalling the ease with which the 1931 disturbances had been crushed. Archbishop Makarios, too, had his reservations concerning the use of force, which he explained to Grivas at meetings on July 10 and August 3, 1951. He felt that sabotage of British military installations might be sufficient to prompt some reconsideration in London of the Cyprus question; and he was very dubious about the value of Grivas' scheme for action by mountain guerrilla bands. Who would they fight there? he asked Grivas. Where were the targets? The British were all in the towns or in bases along the coast. Grivas replied that the presence of guerrillas in the mountains would soon draw the enemy's fire. "Neither of us imagined," Makarios said later, "that the work which we began that summer would not be completed for a decade." [3]

Although he was now firmly committed to the use of force, the Archbishop still hoped to spur the inert Greek government into political action, and to this end he visited Athens regularly. On one such occasion, on July 2, 1952, he secretly attended a meeting of the Loizides committee, which had reduced its membership and bestowed upon itself the title of "Sacred Liberation Committee." It gathered at the home of Professor Dimitris Vezanis, another old comrade from "X", which had previously been disbanded, and who now taught at the Pantheon School of Political Studies. This German-educated don had long been a friend of both Grivas and Makarios, whom he had helped to organize the Enosis plebiscite two years before. He seated the Archbishop at the head of his drawing-room table, around which were ranged some new faces: General Papadopoulos, who had won renown in the war with Italy; Colonel Alexopolos, formerly of the counterespionage service; Professor Konidaris, of Athens University; and Antonios Avgikos, a prominent lawyer. Makarios had said that their committee need number no more than five, and now it had eight members, but some good sense emerged from the rhetorical exchanges. The chief question was whether they should attempt an immediate onslaught against the British or, for a while, resort to diplomatic channels. For two hours they pursued this problem, with Grivas expounding his plan for a twin attack by guerrillas and sabotage groups, while Makarios held that more groundwork must be laid before any armed revolt could succeed. At one point he said to Grivas, "Not fifty men will follow you to the mountains." Grivas replied that he knew the Cypriots: "I am sure they will respond to our call!" Admiral Stratos interposed that while [men are not] born brave, "They can become brave if bravely led."

As an interim step, it was decided that the Archbishop should make a fresh appeal to Greece's leaders before the next meeting of the Liberation Committee. He did so, and found them unenthusiastic about making an appeal to the United Nations. The coalition government, beset with problems after the Nazi occupation and the civil war, was about to break up, and Field Marshal Alexander Papagos, leader of the opposition, waited in the wings to take power.

The Liberation Committee met again on July 21 to hear Makarios' report on his interviews. Since nothing had been gained at those meetings from the political end, it was now agreed the time had come for action. Two committees were set up to study the practical problems of starting the revolution. Stratos, in Makarios' absence, would preside over both committees and coordinate their efforts. Meanwhile, renewed pressure must be brought to bear in Athens. In a farewell broadcast to the nation, on his way to the United Nations, the Archbishop openly denounced both government and opposition:

> They have shown neither boldness nor courage. To the nation's demand for an appeal to the United Nations they have answered in a hesitating and half-hearted fashion that "they are watching the situation closely. . . ." The political leadership fools itself. What is worse, it fools the Greek people; and it also fools the unfortunate Cypriots when it talks of an open door for friendly talks. The British are not your friends. As long as they keep your Cypriot brothers under the yoke, they are not your friends. . . .[4]

This startling attack, over the government-controlled radio, was concluded by an urging to the Greek people to "make your political leaders comply with your demand to bring the Cyprus question before General Assembly . . . to you I entrust the handling of the sacred cause of Cyprus from the Greek side."

Venizelos was angered at this challenge, made through his own mouthpiece; it was understandable, but moot: the government of Venizelos fell, and Marshal Papagos succeeded him, his party winning two hundred thirty-nine of the three hundred parliamentary seats. At last Greece had an administration sufficiently strong to take action over Cyprus, if it had the will.

Grivas set out on a second reconnaissance of Cyprus in October 1952. He stayed first at his brother's house on Alexander the Great Street in the heart of Nicosia. He found Makarios preparing for a visit to New York to publicize the Cyprus cause among delegates to the United Nations in advance of the debate. Before he left, he promised to leave funds for revolutionary preparations with Savvas Loizides in Athens.

Grivas set out on renewed surveys of the mountain areas, climbing Mt. Olympus—at six thousand four hundred feet the highest peak in the Troodos—and the Pentadactylos (Five Fingers) summits of the Kyrenia range. These expeditions deepened his conviction that guerrilla action in the mountains was possible on a limited scale. But the first move would be to organize a campaign of sabotage and surprise attacks by urban guerrillas in the towns.

In Nicosia, Grivas met his first would-be guerrilla fighters: youths recruited from two organizations founded by the Archbishop—OXEN (Young People's Christian Orthodox Union) and PEON (Pancyprian National Youth Organization). The first was headed by Stavros Papa Agathangelos, a middle-aged priest and teacher, who had pioneered its work from Sunday school beginnings. The second, the more militant PEON, was in the hands of Stavros Poskottis, a young teacher. PEON was banned by the British in June 1953, but it continued to operate underground and formed the seedbed of the guerrilla movement.

Of manpower there would be no lack; the next step was to bring in arms, for there were few, aside from sporting guns, in Cyprus. Grivas, before leaving Athens, had arranged for a small caique, bearing an innocent cargo of clay pots and barrels of olives, to make a trial run along the route that arms-smuggling vessels must take. A vessel and a captain had been found by the Loizides brothers.

The caique *St. Irene* sailed from Athens on December 23, arriving on January 1, 1953 at Paphos harbor on the west coast. Stavros Poskottis went down to meet the crew. At once, the little town began to buzz with gossip. The head of PEON, seen talking to a captain and his men from Greece! The news quickly reached the ears of the police, who closely questioned Poskottis and the sailors; then the caique was searched. Only pots and olives were found but the *St. Irene* was asked to leave immediately and a frightened Poskottis returned to Nicosia. This fiasco gave Grivas the opportunity to impress on his collaborators the need for absolute secrecy. It was a lesson the spontaneous Greek Cypriots found hard to learn.

Grivas now turned to a young man who had come knocking on his door in Alexander the Great Street one night in November: this was Andreas Azinas, a young official of PEK, the Farmers Union, who had been sent to him by the Archbishop. Azinas was lively and intelligent—in contrast to the rather dour Poskottis. A student from Salonika University, Azinas had met the Loizides brothers at the Cyprus ethnarchy office in Athens, and he was a close friend of Gregoris Afxentiou, another young Cypriot serving in the Greek army, who was later to become the great hero of the rebellion.

Impressed by the urgency of Azinas' belief in an armed uprising,

Grivas disclosed that he was seeking a spot on the coast where a smuggling caique could land. Azinas suggested a district on the lonely west coast near Paphos, where his family owned land, and fishing trawlers went unnoticed. He drew a sketch map showing the beach, paths, and houses to which the guns could be rapidly transported.

In a score of ways Azinas made himself useful to Grivas: he replaced his small survey map with a British military chart that covered a dozen sheets; he spoke excellent English, and understood the British mentality, thanks largely to the two years he had spent in agricultural studies at Reading University, where he had run the gamut of English university life.

Almost at once Andreas Azinas became Grivas' right-hand man: his position in PEK, permitting him to roam the island unsuspected, his intimacy with Makarios, and his energy made him invaluable. He could drive Grivas from dawn to dusk about the island, attending meetings of the Farmers Union at a dozen villages en route, and still be talking, cogently and cheerfully, as they drove back to the capital toward midnight. Grivas asked Azinas to give up his work and studies to help organize the revolt, in particular the smuggling of arms. He must come with him to Athens. This was agreed.

The visa permitting Grivas' stay in Cyprus as a naturalized Greek citizen expired in January 1953, but he obtained an extension through his brother Michael, after receiving a certificate of poor health from the British-run general hospital.

He used the time to draft a plan for Makarios in which he set out the principles on which an armed revolt would be conducted. It was a document at once precise in its requirements and extensive in its predictions. Grivas stated the aim of an armed revolt as being not to expel the British from Cyprus, or to defeat them, but "to draw the attention of international public opinion" by harassing the British. The revolutionaries must show that there would be no end to the struggle until the U.N. had examined the problem and the diplomats had reached a settlement in accordance with Cypriot and Greek desires. The aim of the revolt would be achieved in three ways: by sabotage of government and military installations; by surprise attacks of highly mobile guerrilla units on British forces; and by organizing the passive resistance of the people.[5]

Grivas noted that the main weight of the campaign would have to lie on sabotage, because "the territory is not capable of absorbing large guerrilla forces." There always came a time when the terrain had to be regarded as having reached "saturation point," and it was essential to discover in practice what that point was. Numerical superiority was irrelevant in guerrilla warfare, Grivas insisted, so long as the right tactics were used and—above all—the men were resourcefully led.

While working out this general plan on paper, he envisaged activities that would be on a larger scale in the mountain areas, and more limited in the treeless plains. But events quickly showed that operations were equally feasible in the flat countryside of the Mesaoria plain around Famagusta. The reasons were that his Famagusta leaders knew the land better than they knew the mountains, they were closer to their hideouts and supply points, they were surrounded by sympathetic villagers, and were led not only with courage but with cunning. The mountain units, on the other hand, often found themselves working in difficult and unfamiliar terrain far from villages and supplies. Cooped up in subterranean hideouts, they could not dissolve into the population and so offered themselves as targets to the British. Still, as Grivas wrote in his plan: "The military task of the combat units will have as its principal aim the cover and support of the saboteurs' work, as well as to confuse and divert the attention of the British administration." Their activities could be increased later, if all went well. Initially, five guerrilla "shock groups" would be set up in the Troodos and Kyrenia ranges, each group numbering from eight to ten men. (The size of these groups was later reduced to five or six.)

Sabotage groups were planned for every town and district: they would use time bombs, dynamite, and mines; and Grivas would personally select the targets and supervise the formation of the groups. Special intelligence centers would be created to watch British troop movements and military targets, and measures would be taken to "punish severely" any Cypriots who acted as British agents. (This in practice almost always meant assassination, and again Grivas personally judged the cases and ordered the execution of "traitors.")

The plan placed enormous importance on public support. Seemingly, Grivas could not emphasize too often or too strongly the need to "neutralize" all opposition, to coordinate the military and civil struggle, to organize passive resistance through a boycott of things British, and to encourage the participation of the young and the students in disturbances. "Who wins over the people," he wrote, "has won half the battle." [6]

Also, in this preliminary plan Grivas devoted a disproportionate amount of space to formation of the mountain guerrillas, although he stated that sabotage would be his chief weapon. The idea of these bands, following in the romantic Hellenic tradition of those that had liberated Greece and Crete from the Turks, and later from their German occupiers in World War II, was dear to his heart.

Grivas returned to Athens on February 23, 1953, and placed his proposals before the Liberation Committee. He set about collecting arms and seeking support for the venture, and to this end, through friends high in the Greek military establishment, he approached Premier Papagos. Papagos' reply was that he had not wished to know of Grivas' plans, and now that he did, no one must know that he knew. For good reason: it was barely a month since he had linked Greece to Turkey in a new pact, and it seemed early to disrupt the accord with an attempt to annex Cyprus.

Archbishop Makarios reached Athens on March 10, at the end of another attempt to "enlighten" U.N. delegates and British politicians. He saw Papagos but obtained from him no more than promises of diplomatic action. Next, he met Grivas and Socrates Loizides at Grivas' small apartment and agreed that they must hasten their revolutionary plans. But again he demurred at Grivas' schemes for mountain guerrillas. He wanted only sabotage, and nonlethal sabotage at that. When Grivas tried to insist, urging the psychological value of these bands to their cause, Makarios stood firm. He told the authors in July 1962:

> I said they could only fight back in self-defense if they found themselves in difficulties. I said that Grivas must take his orders from me as Ethnarch and leader of the political struggle. We would discuss everything, but I would have the final word. He promised this, and obeyed for as long as I was in Cyprus.

For Grivas, it was highly frustrating; but worse was in store. Makarios said that the "arms" were to consist only of explosives; guns he did not want. Nor was Grivas to send any Greek to Cyprus; this should be a purely Cypriot revolution.

Grivas retorted in anger that it would be better if he dropped out of the whole affair rather than agree to tactics that would inevitably destroy the campaign. The Liberation Committee warmly supported him, and there was even talk of "going ahead without Makarios." Faced with such a consensus, the Archbishop relented and advised Grivas, through his brother, that he might prepare such material for dispatch as he saw fit; at the same time more money was made available through Savvas Loizides.

Premier Papagos' hopes of a friendly approach to Britain were dispelled by a meeting on September 22, 1953, with Sir Anthony Eden, who was convalescing on a Mediterranean cruise after a severe illness. The British foreign secretary refused to discuss the subject: for his government, as for the preceding Labour administrations, the Enosis question did not exist. The exchange was blunt and brief, and Papagos came away with wounded pride.[7]

On November 27, 1953, Papagos announced that he would be personally handling the Cyprus question, and Greece was firmly set on a collision course with Britain at the United Nations.

Revolutionary preparations now proceeded with more speed. Azinas—created secretary-general of PEK so that he might more easily travel in Cyprus and abroad—had chosen landing points for the arms caiques, and selected a team of trusted men to meet them. Grivas had gathered a modest store of arms and explosives and made an important new addition to the committee: an admiral of the Royal Hellenic Navy who would help them to find a caique and a captain, make arrangements for the voyage, advise on naval matters, and see that the appropriate authorities turned a blind eye.

Admiral M. Sakelariou was radically Anglophile—he had served alongside Britain's commander-in-chief, Admiral John Cunningham in the Mediterranean, and had been awarded the K.C.B., the highest British decoration ever bestowed on a Greek officer—but he could not, as a Greek, refuse to assist in liberating a Greek island from the British. And as a former minister of defense and vice premier of the Greek government in exile during the occupation, he still wielded much influence in Athens.

The Liberation Committee agreed on January 28, 1954, to start action as soon as possible. Already it seemed probable that British forces would soon be obliged to leave Suez, as a result of terrorism there; then they would fall back on Cyprus and flood the island with troops.

When Archbishop Makarios arrived in Athens on February 15, Grivas at once urged him to permit an immediate shipment of arms to Cyprus and the start of hostilities.

The material had been assembled chiefly by former members of "X" headed by George Gazouleas and the brothers Michael and Constantine Efstathopolous, both lawyers. Most of the guns had come from Greek army stores, through Liberation Committee members serving in the forces. A brigadier named Xintaras had been especially helpful. A few well-wishers also contributed: a former resistance fighter, now a newspaper editor, had given up a German Staiger machine gun with thirteen clips of ammunition. Gazouleas handed over his personal revolver. To these were added the somewhat dilapidated guns of ''X''—weapons of all ages, bores, and nationalities. The grand total finally dispatched to the port of Piraeus consisted of twenty-nine automatics and machine guns, forty-seven rifles, seven revolvers, more than thirty-two thousand bullets, two hundred and ninty hand grenades, and twenty kilos of explosive. The total cost of purchase, packing, and transport was fifty thousand drachmae—about one thousand four hundred and fifty dollars. The Church of Cyprus paid this sum, as it paid all other bills of the revolution.

The material was moved in two lorries to Lavrion, a small harbor on the Attic coast. Gazouleas was waiting with a loading party. The caique *Siren* lay off shore, under the skipper chosen by Admiral Sakelariou—Captain Evangelos Koutalianos, a man with an impressive war record. In his cabin hung a certificate issued by British GHQ, Middle East, thanking him for his work in smuggling arms and agents into occupied Greece.

The *Siren* took the crates safely aboard, and by dawn was well out to sea. March storms forced her to take refuge at the islands of Koufonistra and Castelorizon during the voyage, and the reception party in Cyprus had almost abandoned hope of her arrival when, on the afternoon of March 25, a caique was seen some miles out. Under cover of darkness, Azinas and his men waited on the beach at Khlorakas, north of Paphos, as they had done every night for the past three weeks. He flashed the agreed signal—three blinks of light every five minutes—and was rewarded by an answering light out to sea. By four in the morning, all forty-five cases had been hauled inland and hidden in prearranged spots: a pumping-house, a tomato patch, a manure heap.

Next morning Azinas telephoned to Savvas Loizides in Athens: ''We have the potato seed.''

— 2 —

Grivas Lands in Cyprus

The Archbishop remained in Athens after the caique's departure to meet King Paul and leaders of the government and urge them toward political action. On March 14, 1954, he was able to announce in a broadcast over Athens radio that he had received from Papagos categorical assurances that the question of Cyprus would be brought before the U.N. General Assembly the following September.

The British government now decided to take a firmer stance over Cyprus. After a long campaign of murder and sabotage by Egyptian revolutionaries, British forces were being withdrawn permanently from their major bases along the Suez Canal. They would fall back on Cyprus, which was to serve as the new bastion of British prestige and influence in the Middle East. Work on costly new British land and air bases was already well under way in July 1954 along the island's southern shores. Tens of thousands of troops were flowing into these bases near Limassol, Larnaca, and Famagusta. And when Labour members of Parliament suggested in the House of Commons that Cyprus, too, might be disrupted by the kind of terrorism that had obliged the retreat from Suez, the idea was rejected by Conservative leaders; their military advisers had examined the possibility and decided that a revolutionary movement had no chance of success. Henry Hopkinson, minister of state for colonial affairs, announced that Cyprus was one of those territories that could never hope to be fully independent because of Britian's defense obligations in the Middle East. He added that he saw no reason to expect any difficulties in Cyprus as result of this decision.

These expectations collapsed when the Greek government promptly lodged the long promised appeal over Cyprus with the United Nations, to the accompaniment of carefully orchestrated student riots in Athens, attacks on British consulates elsewhere in Greece, and strikes on Cyprus.

Amid this growing agitation for Enosis, British police and military intelligence could not remain wholly unaware. An effort was made to strengthen the Cyprus Police Special Branch, a body of select British and Cypriot officers whose main task was to investigate political unrest and sedition. Intelligence experts came out from Britain to assist in reorganizing the Special Branch. Agents were planted at meetings of Cypriot nationalist organizations, and Cypriots prominent in the Enosis movement were watched. The British picked up rumors that some kind of underground organization—perhaps modeled on Grivas' wartime band "X"—was being formed. The Cyprus government drew up a list of trouble makers and other "undesirables" which included Grivas' name. Thus when Grivas once more applied to the British embassy in Athens for a visa, he was refused. To his exasperation, he must now arrange a clandestine entry into the island, a project that might be hampered by friction among the conspirators in Athens. For one such encounter, Grivas was himself to blame: he kept a diary, in which he recorded with great detail and candor the progress of the struggle and his opinions of the participants. Savvas Loizides, happening across this one day on a desk, read it and discovered an entry that accused him of "reluctance" to begin the uprising. Liozides confronted Grivas in a rage: suppose such a monstrous lie was written into history? It took the combined diplomatic arts of the other plotters to heal the rift.

Despite these tribulations, preparation of a second arms caique had gone ahead with money made available by Makarios, who stopped in Athens through the first weeks of October before flying to New York for the U.N. debate. The Archbishop met Grivas several times. It was agreed that Grivas should leave for Cyprus as soon as possible, and also that there should be action only if the debate went against them. Makarios promised to send permission to start the revolt from the United States.

Grivas decided that for security reasons he should go ahead of the second arms caique in a passenger steamer to Rhodes, where the little *Siren* would be waiting to carry him on the last lap to Cyprus. On October 26, 1954, he set out, carrying a suitcase that held a few clothes, a stout pair of boots, field glasses and his Smith-Webley revolver. With Socrates Loizides, he sailed at four in the afternoon aboard the *Aegean*.

They disembarked in pouring rain the following afternoon. At a waterfront cafe the captain of the *Siren* shrugged aside Grivas' demands that they should leave at once. Two caiques had gone down in this storm, and he did not intend to risk his thirty-foot coastal fishing boat or its crew of three. Huge waves were bursting over the jetty, breaking high on the lighthouse.

For most of their stay on Rhodes, the two men lived furtively in a bare rented room of what had once been a Masonic lodge, sleeping on the floor and living on canned food. In these frustrating circumstances another quarrel broke out: Socrates Loizides saw the movement as being led by a triumvirate in which he was the third party. When Grivas abruptly disabused him of this idea, a dispute began that ended with Grivas stalking out to other quarters at the Rhodes tourist office. Socrates sulked for six days, while the stormy weather continued, threatening to return to Athens; but at last reason prevailed, and the quarrel was patched up.

They were joined by Notis Petropouleas, the man Grivas had chosen as his aide; he had served in the Greek army and would be useful in training men. Petropouleas was young, tall, and dashing. Socrates took an immediate dislike to him.

Not until November 8 did the weather clear. Thirteen days had been lost. Toward midnight they embarked from a small, rocky bay, wading out in a heavy swell in pitch darkness to the dinghy. A sailor took Grivas on his back, but Socrates and Notis—their suitcases on their heads—were almost up to their necks in water before they reached the boat.

A few hours out to sea on the 200-mile journey, a fresh storm struck. The small craft wallowed horribly. Grivas was flung about the captain's boxlike cabin, while Socrates and Notis clung to ropes on decks awash with icy water. They were all violently sick.

Grivas rejected the captain's suggestion that they take refuge at the island of Castelorizon off the Turkish coast. The straining engine broke down. For hours they rolled and pitched as the crew attempted to make repairs, hampered by waves that washed over the sides. The buffeting continued through the second day at sea. Grivas appeared at times to be unconscious.

On the afternoon of the third day the storm abated. Almost at once they sighted Cape Arnauti, at the northwest tip of Cyprus. As daylight faded they sailed south toward Paphos. The lights of the little town shone as they dropped anchor a mile or two off shore. At nine in the evening a flashlight beamed red then green on the beach below Khlorakas village. Sailors rowed Grivas and his companions ashore. Grivas shook hands with the three villagers, relatives of Azinas, who greeted them, then marched up and down the beach to bring the circulation back to his legs. The moon came out. The wind was still.

"Is this another world here?" Grivas asked. They were taken to a village house and fed with soup and chicken. Grivas would not eat the meat, and old Mrs. Azinas thought he looked readier for the grave than for a revolution. They could always bury him secretly in the little cemetery up the road, she suggested to her husband.

Grivas assured himself that the arms sent on ahead were still safe. then he slept. For three days he did not leave the house. Meals were carried in to him as he studied maps, wrote letters, made plans and filled the pages of a small pocket notebook which was his diary. At the end of the three days he was ready for action. He wrote:

> 13th Nov. 1954: In the evening the training of five men of the Khlorakas group was started with automatics and sabotage. Duration from 1900 to 2300 hours. . . .[1]

The guns which had been transported in the first caique were brought from their hiding places and cleaned, and the villagers stripped the grease from each weapon, replaced it with a light film of oil, then packed guns and explosives into cars for distribution about the island.

Grivas and Notis gave the Cypriots, most of whom had never held an automatic weapon, some arms training. Then they were made to place their hands on a Bible and swear "in the name of the Holy Trinity" to work for the liberation of Cyprus, sacrificing their lives if necessary; to obey "the Leader's" orders unquestioningly, and never to reveal the organization's secrets on pain of punishment.[2]

Socrates had angered Grivas by moping over the photograph of his wife Chloe, whom he had married a few days before leaving Athens, and repeatedly remarking how much he missed her. "Did he think we were going to a wedding?" asked Grivas.

Grivas sent Socrates to an isolated village to see what could be done about organizing the important district of Limassol, while he himself headed for the capital by car. En route they made detours to inspect the new bases of British Middle East Headquarters. The first advance parties had already arrived, and barracks, airfields, power stations, and colonies of little identical houses—the military's "married quarters"—were going up. On an unsurfaced road, the car's back wheels sank axle-deep in mud. But soon an army lorry appeared and soldiers hauled them out and directed them through their camp. They drove on along the south coast, past the great new bases going up at Dhekelia, near Larnaca, a signals center with towering radio masts outside Famagusta, and reached Nicosia. Grivas inspected the law courts and the Secretariat compound, the seat of government, with a view to sabotage. He considered the day well spent. Now he would make his base in the capital.

From a small house on the outskirts of Nicosia, Grivas began organizing the first sabotage groups, with Notis as his aide. After a week, he had three groups of young saboteurs—eighteen men in all—drawn from PEON, and others with some rudimentary training in the use of guns from OXEN. Several of those he met were to become leaders of the organization: Polycarpos Georgadjis, Markos Drakos, Stylianos Lenas— all became guerrilla or area chiefs. No one but Notis or Azinas came to Grivas' headquarters. In these early days, Grivas drove freely about the town, taking few precautions. He allowed only a handful of confederates to know where he lived. Not even the head of OXEN was brought there: Grivas drove out to meet him on a lonely country road, and they sat talking in the back of the car for an hour.

In December, Grivas heard the first news from the U.N., over the government-controlled Cyprus Broadcasting Service. Staffed by colonial civil servants, CBS worked to counter Enosis and play down the U.N. appeal. Grivas confided to his diary:

> 16th Dec. 1954: The first news from the U.N. is unfavorable to Greece. America's position is against us and after this we should expect nothing from the U.N. . . . . Our wise diplomats who were boasting that a solution would be found through the U.N., what do they intend to do now? Churchill . . . arranged everything with Eisenhower. It was obvious. . . .[3]

The United States had supported the British desire to avoid discussion of the Cyprus issue. The U.N. had resolved that "for the time being, it does not appear appropriate to adopt a resolution." There were disturbances in Greece and Cyprus at this decision, but Grivas held his hand, waiting for a signal from Makarios that never came. The conspirators were puzzled; only weeks before, the Archbishop had promised to send instructions.

But a worse blow lay in store. Since late November, they had worried over the nonappearance of the caique that was to have followed Grivas out with the second load of arms. Night after night, Azinas' party waited on the beach, where they noticed perturbing signs of police and military presence in this usually deserted area. Finally the Athenian conspirators called Azinas urgently to Greece. He was soon back, to report that all the arms were lost: the crew of the caique, alarmed by the sight of "unidentifiable" lights along the west coast, had thrown them into the sea and fled. The captain had been paid in full, after falsely reporting safe delivery of the cargo of the explosives they urgently needed for sabotage operations: one thousand pounds of dynamite and other explosive materials; thirty-four pistols, one hundred mines, three hundred grenades, and eight thousand rounds of ammunition—all had gone to the bottom.

Once again the smugglers in Athens turned to Captain Koutalianos, who had safely delivered the first load of arms in March. He undertook to charter a new caique, the *St. George*. Paid with an advance of one hundred and ninety British gold sovereigns—for paper money, given the ruinous state of the Greek economy, was unacceptable—Koutalianos equipped the vessel for the run, even down to a Turkish flag.

But more cash was required for the purchase of guns, and this awaited the return of the Archbishop from the United Nations. He reached Athens on December 29 and at once inquired of Azinas, with some asperity, why there had been no action in Cyprus. Azinas was astonished: had not His Beatitude cabled instructions to wait? Makarios had not. Inquiry revealed that Greece's U.N. delegate, Alexis Kyrou, had signaled the Greek consul in Nicosia to this effect without the Archbishop's knowledge, doubtless with his government's approval, and almost certainly with the connivance of Savvas Loizides, who had heard rumors of the quarrels in Cyprus and wished his brother placed beyond range of Grivas' wrath. Savvas thought Socrates unsuited for military glory and wanted him returned to Greece. The Archbishop agreed that Socrates should return aboard the *St. George*, when she had deposited her next load of arms. To this end he now produced a further three thousand dollars—three-quarters of which would go to Koutalianos, the rest to purchase arms. Gazouleas had gathered another score of revolvers, two automatics, and a dozen grenades; while the obliging Brigadier Xintaras, who was on the board of a munitions factory, secured another one thousand pounds of explosive, fuses, and detonators. Xintaras simply signed orders for the destruction of these stores owing to their decayed condition, to cover up the deal.

In Nicosia, Grivas had chosen and personally inspected the first targets for attack, as he drove through the Secretariat and past Wolseley Barracks, the army headquarters. On New Year's Eve, the sabotage groups reconnoitered their targets—the CBS studios and two nearby military radio stations.

— 3 —

Capture of the *St. George*

The British community on Cyprus was, of course, wholly unaware of the revolutionary rehearsals taking place; they welcomed in the New Year in traditional style at a hundred parties, none more popular than that of the Nicosia Club, a British institution with golf course, tennis courts, and swimming pool. The festivities were thus reported by the *Cyprus Mail:*

> Nearly 300 members of the Club, the majority clad in weird and wonderful fancy dress costumes and disguises ushered in the New Year with song and dance to the music of the Royal Inniskilling Fusiliers. It was a gay and colourful scene with everyone in the highest spirits, which went on until the very early hours of the morning.[1]

The British administration had nonetheless received some indication that an underground movement was being planned, on a very minor scale, it seemed. There had been rumors of caiques, two feeble attempts at sabotage, and attempts to cut the power supply to Government House during the last celebration of the Queen's birthday. The police force was small, ill-trained, and underpaid.[2] Radio communication was nonexistent, transport inadequate, and many isolated police posts had no telephone. And the revolutionaries had their agents in the police.

Police Constable Pavlos Stokkos, an enthusiastic nationalist whose father had been prominent in the 1931 uprising, worked in the Special Branch publications department, and there he saw a secret circular addressed to district police commanders:

> The fact that an organisation in Greece might take an active part in Cyprus over the Enosis question was brought to the fore when informa-

30

tion was received from a previously untested informant that Colonel Grivas, a Cypriot-born naturalised Greek subject who had been refused entry in June this year, had succeeded in landing secretly in Cyprus. . . .

Stokkos passed this on through contacts in the Church to the Archbishop, adding some notes on British intelligence precautions.

Makarios had just returned to Cyprus from New York, via Athens, where he had consulted with Papagos, who now wanted action. Meeting with Grivas on the day after his arrival, Makarios explained that Papagos was now in agreement with their plans. The Archbishop had decided that they should start the revolt on March 25, Greek Independence Day.[3] Grivas said that was too late. The advantage of surprise attack was vital. Government and military installations were at present almost totally unguarded, but that would not last. They left the decision open. Finally, Grivas explained his progress in organizing the movement. The Archbishop said that if anything should happen to him, the bishop of Kitium was his deputy; Grivas replied that Azinas was his.

Later, Grivas wrote in his diary:

> Jan. 11, '55: What a terrible thing it is when politicians and, worse still, men in charge of governments, react in this manner to matters of national importance and make use of them for their own party interests! Instead of Papagos supporting us—behind the scenes at any event—he has been restraining us until today, and anything we have done we have done in spite of him since all has been accomplished by me and my collaborators . When Papagos was put before the accomplished fact of all that had been done and when he was faced with the impasse of the UNO [U.N.] decision, he was forced to change his mind. But what help has he given us? None! [4]

On the following Sunday—anniversary of the famous 1950 Enosis plebiscite—the Archbishop made his traditional fighting speech to a crowd that filled the square around Phaneromeni Cathedral in Nicosia, harping on a theme that was to become a consuming problem of the revolution: treachery. "We are confident," said the Archbishop, "that no Greek Cypriot will be found to become a traitor for any sum of money," . . . but, he warned, British agents were organizing an intelligence network to spy on the Enosis movement, and they would be seeking "spies and mercenary traitors" to infiltrate Cypriot ranks. Let the people beware!

But despite the warning the first of a long line of spies and traitors—
later to be executed by the hundred on Grivas' orders—had already been
found. On January 5, a week before the *St. George* was to sail for
Cyprus with the second cargo of arms expected by Grivas, the British
chief of police, Commissioner G. H. Robins, warned his top man in
Paphos, Assistant Superintendent Alexis Ioannou, that information had
been received from intelligence agents in Athens about a gun-running
caique that would soon sail for Cyprus.

The *St. George* left Athens on January 13, loaded with forty-five cases
of arms and explosives. That day Commissioner Robins told Ioannou
that the caique could be expected at any time next week: he must capture the smugglers and the reception party on the beach. A destroyer,
H.M.S. *Charity,* would plot the caique's course on radar. RAF reconnaissance flights and high speed launches would be available.

Captain Koutalianos and his three-man crew sailed toward the trap.
Azinas had received the signal from Athens: "Thirteen cases have left,"
and every night his party was on the beach at Khlorakas awaiting it.
Then, through Stokkos, they learned that they had been betrayed. Examining the Special Branch wastepaper baskets, Stokkos had discovered
the stencil of a "top secret" signal warning district police chiefs of the
caique's imminent arrival. He passed it on to the Archbishop's aides.

Grivas had the news next morning. He dispatched Azinas at once to
Paphos for a first-hand investigation before any decision were made,
and confided to his diary: ". . . I have been worrying my head all day
trying to think who could have been the traitor. Is he a Greek? My only
hopes are now in God! He who has been my guide until today will continue helping me. I believe this. . . ." [5]

Divine intervention, however, was slow in coming; and for the next
ten days and nights police and rebels kept watch upon the coast and
upon each other. Azinas sent Grivas a written report:

Dear Leader,
. . . we found definite information that the police have been alerted.
Five Special Branch men arrived from Nicosia in the afternoon. The
Army's radar is in constant operation, sweeping over a 15-mile ra-
dius. . . . [6]

At Paphos, both British and Cypriot reception parties were losing patience. The Navy had other duties for H.M.S. *Charity* and only after a

direct appeal to the Admiralty in London was a replacement obtained; this was the destroyer H.M.S. *Comet.*

Socrates Loizides went every night with the Cypriot party to the beach. On January 25, a moonless, cloudy night, the *Comet's* radar screens picked up a caique, moving south at six knots, toward the suspected beach. At last the dot on the radar screen merged with the shoreline, and almost simultaneously the green light began to flash from the land. The destroyer's commander radioed Paphos police station, and Ioannou and his men raced off to grab the landing party.

They quickly overpowered the lookouts, then peered over the cliff edge at the beach, where shadowy figures moved. Ioannou sent two parties of men round to the other side of the cove, waiting until he heard a dinghy's keel grind on the beach. He shouted: "Hands up, everyone! We are police. Wait where you are for my orders or we'll fire!"

In the beam of flashlights, men raised their arms. A voice called up: "We're not armed. You needn't shoot!"

As the prisoners were led away, the sound of gunfire came from the sea. H.M.S. *Comet* had fired a shot across the bow of the *St. George,* which was desperately trying to escape, as the crew hurled crates of arms over the side. The destroyer's searchlights fixed the caique in their beams and a Cypriot policeman hailed the captain in Greek, threatening to sink his ship if he continued to run.

Captain Koutalianos saw that the situation was hopeless, he cut out the engine, and the *St. George* came to a stop within two hundred yards. A boarding party handcuffed the crew.

On the beach and in the caique were thirty boxes labeled DANGER— EXPLOSIVES, containing some ten thousand sticks of dynamite. Trampled into the sand police found a receipt for money signed by Azinas, which Loizides had tried and failed to destroy by swallowing. Now Azinas, Grivas' top aide, was a wanted man—his offices in Nicosia were searched and records of his numerous trips to Athens discovered. As for the *St. George,* she was towed to Paphos, where she sat for months in the harbor with the Union Jack hanging from her mast.

It was a stunning blow for Grivas: much more than the arms had been lost—there could be no surprise attack now. The whole movement was endangered. He wrote in his diary:

26 Jan.'55: . . . who was it who gave us away? May our own curses and those of Cyprus weigh heavily upon him! There will always be trai-

tors, but I had not imagined that there could be in this particular instance
Greeks whose love for money overrides all else. We are stubbornly determined to continue the struggle even with our reduced means. . . . I am
closing my diary at this point and I shall hide it in case it should fall into
enemy hands. Hard times, these!

The "means" were indeed reduced: two cargoes lost, and no hope
now of bringing in a third. They must attempt to begin the fight with
twenty kilos of explosive, two hundred and ninety World War II hand
grenades, and eighty-three obsolete guns. "It seems," wrote the Archbishop to Grivas, "that we have lost before we have started." [7]

— 4 —

The Revolt Begins

Grivas decided to leave Nicosia until the *St. George* scare would have died down. He buried his diary and papers in glass jars in the earth, and moved to the village of Kakopetria, high in the Troodos range. Once again, his mind was dwelling on the vision of guerrilla fighting in the mountains, where a small group was being formed. Grivas refused to let the caique's loss depress him. He wrote to Makarios:

> . . . it has hardened our hearts, so that with greater will-power, sacrifice and stubbornness we will move forward to liberate Cyprus. I am speaking not only for myself but also on behalf of those whom I have the honour to command and amongst whom I now happen to be. . . .

He needed money in the mountains for couriers, arms, and ammunition. Guerrilla action, he went on,

> will play the greater part of the combined action because our material possibilities from such activities are greater than from sabotage. . . . You must have complete trust in me.[1]

The Archbishop had no faith in the notion of armed bands roving the mountains looking for British troops that were not there. He called Grivas back to a meeting in Nicosia, at the Metochi, or annex, of Kykko monastery, a rambling collection of modern sandstone buildings centering on a small church in a cobbled courtyard. They met in the abbot's private study.

Makarios was critical of Grivas' security arrangements, which had proved inadequate in the recent capture of the *St. George,* but Grivas swore the leak had occurred in Athens: how else could the British know the caique was on the way on the very day she sailed—even before the conspirators in Cyprus knew? At least, said Makarios, the prisoners had not betrayed them, nor were the police following up their success.

As for the start of activities, the Archbishop still wanted minimal sabotage and no bloodshed. Grivas wrote later in his diary:

> 31st Jan. '55: . . . he precluded active guerrilla operations for the present and said that military objectives should be attacked, but without inflicting casualties. He did not approve of my suggestion of parallel action by guerrilla groups, and I was forced to comply.[2]

For the next two months Grivas stayed in Nicosia, devoting his energies to preparing the first attacks. He often had occasion to berate idle or untrustworthy subordinates. Few measured up to his relentless standards, but he did cast a hopeful eye over a young man named Gregoris Afxentiou. Afxentiou, a student from Greece, was a lieutenant in the Greek Army Reserve, although a Cypriot by birth. Azinas, a friend of Afxentiou for several years, had introduced him to Grivas at Lyssi village, where Afxentiou worked his father's land. Grivas was impressed by Afxentiou's revolutionary spirit. He told the young man he wanted him to lead sabotage missions in the Famagusta area. His three years of military training would be invaluable.

With the caique lost, Grivas sought supplies inside the island. It was Afxentiou who found them. His source of supply was the seabed.

In 1946, the British army had dumped two hundred tons of deteriorating mines and shells off the Famagusta coast. Ever since, Cypriot fishermen had hauled them up for use in the illegal but profitable business of fishing with dynamite. The British had failed to calculate the strength of local currents, and scores of shells had been washed into shallow water a few hundred yards off shore. Afxentiou reported that round, cake-shaped land mines, weighing between five and eight pounds, and 3.7 inch anti-aircraft shells could be purchased for prices between ten shillings and three pounds. Swimmers, trained in diving without oxygen equipment, could do the work by daylight with little danger of interference.

One rich mine bed lay off a deserted beach near the ruins of Salamis, the early Greek settlement. Other explosives came from shells which boys collected after every firing from the British military ranges and sold. Dynamite was stolen from the mines, where it was used for blasting. For all these purchases the Archbishop supplied the cash.

By the end of February, Grivas had ample material to start operations. He listed in his diary the stores gathered by his Famagusta team. It included more than two hundred sticks of dynamite, a score of mines, hundreds of feet of fuse and metal piping for the manufacture of home-made grenades, and a few guns bought here and there. Several thousand pounds of prepared explosive were garnered over the space of a year before the British cut off the supply. By then the organization was manufacturing its own explosives from locally available chemicals.

Slowly the movement took shape. A first order went out to district commanders on February 8, stressing basic rules. Of these, the first and most important was that only Grivas gave orders. Local leaders could, however, select their own rank-and-file in five categories: demonstrators; townspeople who would harbor wanted men; saboteurs and guerrillas; agents in the police and in army camps (which employed much Cypriot labor); and counterspies to watch government agents (usually Cypriot civil servants in the lower grades of the Secretariat).

From the outset, Grivas tried to instill in his inexperienced followers a few principles of secrecy, emphasizing that disobedience must be severely punished. Members should be unknown to other members as far as possible. Reliable couriers should be found to link the groups. District leaders should send full weekly reports on missions and targets. So far, he had appointed four leaders: Afxentiou for Famagusta; Notis for Lamassol; Stavros Poskottis for Larnaca; and Evangelos Evangelakis for Nicosia. They were an unlikely team to start a revolution. Poskottis was a schoolmasterly intellectual; Evangelakis, a young PEON worker; Notis, an army sergeant turned adventurer. Afxentiou alone offered a suitable blend of expertise and daring; and only he was to continue to lead after the first few weeks of action.

Notis inspected Government House, with sabotage in view. A Cypriot named Michaelopolis who had worked there as a clerk for twelve years, from 1941 to 1954, seeing out five British governors, took him round the great house. The Cypriot staff were indifferent to the visitors; the British were unaware that they were not part of the numerous Cypriot staff. Notis reported to Grivas that the bedrooms would provide an excellent spot in which to plant a bomb.

Notis was enterprising but all too casual. Guns were sent to the wrong destination. He spent much time with a dancer from a local cabaret, and Grivas peppered his diary with notes about unpaid grocer's bills for the group, running into hundreds of dollars.

On March 7 Makarios and Grivas met again to discuss the date of their first attack. The Archbishop agreed that action should start after his preferred date—March 25—since the British might be prepared for trouble on Greek Independence Day; and now, at last, matters went ahead with greater speed. More explosives were found: mines, bullets, a barrel of amatol (a potent mixture of TNT and ammonium nitrate). Leaders were giving instruction to their teams. The Secretariat, the open government compound of offices and stores, shaded by eucalyptus trees, on the edge of Nicosia, was reconnoitered for places to plant bombs.

On March 8 Grivas wrote:

> It is possible to undertake these targets because we have obtained more material. . . . Thank God, at last. Something will be achieved with God's help.[3]

His final list of targets throughout the island included in Nicosia CBS and FBS, the government and British Forces radio stations, Wolseley Barracks, the Secretariat, and the Education office; in Famagusta, Limassol, and Larnaca, a variety of police and power stations, courthouses, and army depots.

Grivas found, in Polycarpos Georgadjis, a young clerk at the Cyprus Chamber of Commerce, an ideal intelligence agent who took pleasure in this secretive type of work. Grivas set him to organize the capital's first intelligence team, with the task of finding houses in which groups could meet, where hideouts could be constructed, and explosives stored. Above all, he was to pick Cypriots in the police and administration who would supply news of British intentions.

Georgadjis (who was later to become minister of the interior in the first Cypriot government) [4] also shipped arms throughout the town in the huge straw market baskets common in Cyprus—with a covering of oranges.

Grivas was now the guest of the former Government House accounts clerk, Michael Michaelopolis, who lived with his wife and children in a house in the suburb of Strovolos. Michaelopolis was a trusted friend of Evangelakis and other PEON members. Grivas ate his meals with the family, but spent the rest of each day alone in a room writing, emerging after dark to pace up and down in the back yard.

Then he moved to a more private house on the edge of Nicosia, a new villa with pebbledash walls. The fact that this area was occupied by many British families would lessen the chance of searches. Across the road, some three hundred yards away, was a police station. This was to be his main headquarters during the next five months.

An official tenant for the house, who would act as cover for Grivas and supply his needs, was required. For this role he chose Pascalis Papadopolis, secretary of a right-wing trade union, and Papadopolis then employed one of his closest friends, a fellow unionist named Yannis Alexandrou, to construct a hideout under the floor. With help from the trusted handful of men in Grivas' immediate circle, they excavated a secret cellar, surfacing it with concrete. A reserve hideout was created in a house at Strovolos.

A final meeting was held with Makarios at Kykko annex on the evening of March 29. Grivas returned to record in his diary:

> WE CAN START. He gave me his blessing. God is with us. I must start as soon as possible because as we go along the moon will hamper us. It is six days old today. Tomorrow I see the section leaders and if they are ready we will start on the night of March 31. . . . I close my book now because I am preparing to bury it.[5]

The notebooks containing the diary were rolled up and squeezed into two glass jars. Grivas told his batman-bodyguard Gregoris Louka to bury them in a safe place. Louka drove to Lyssi, his home town, and hid them in the earth on family land. These copious diaries, kept from a date in autumn of 1954 and continued throughout the revolution—even after some were discovered by the British in 1956—record Grivas' candid opinions of his fellow conspirators and give a detailed picture of the organization he had created. It seems surprising today that a man so conscious of the need for secrecy would commit to paper so many facts that would yield valuable intelligence for the British.[6] But Grivas' experience of the politicians in Athens had been bitter; and he doubted if he could trust Makarios when the time came for a historical reckoning. These considerations outweighed the risk of discovery. As he warned Makarios in a letter on April 2, 1955:

> If I survive I shall have many things to speak about everybody and about what they have contributed in this struggle. If I die I shall leave them in writing.[7]

Grivas summoned his four chief lieutenants, Petropouleas, Afxentiou, Evangelakis, and Poskottis to a joint conference, informing them that action would start at 0030 hours on April 1. He read aloud his first "revolutionary proclamation"—a leaflet which had been multigraphed for distribution:

> Brother Cypriots, from the depths of past centuries all those who glorified Greek history to preserve their freedom are watching us: the warriors of Marathon, the warriors of Salamis, the 300 of Leonidas. . . . Let us be worthy of them. It is time to show the world that if national diplomacy is unjust and cowardly, the soul of a Cypriot is brave. . . . Forward altogether for freedom . . . ! [8]

The leaflet was signed, "EOKA—the Leader—Dighenis." EOKA was the name he had chosen for the organization, with Makarios' agreement. The initials stood for Ethniki Organosis Kyprion Agoniston (National Organization of Cypriot Fighters). Dighenis Akritas is a folk hero of Byzantine legend. The declaration reduced all present, including its author, to tears. Grivas embraced each man in turn and fervently wished all good luck.

On the night of the attack, Grivas wrote in his diary:

> The time of activity is drawing near. At 0030 I noticed a short interruption of the current but without any other result. What has happened? Has the attempt to cut off the current failed?
> Some minutes after 0030 hours the first explosions are heard. They are followed by others and finally the last one, which is also the biggest. We went to bed at 0300 hours. We shall know the results tomorrow. [9]

In his palace at the heart of the old town, Archbishop Makarios burnt in his study fireplace all incriminating letters. On hearing the first explosions, he went out on the balcony. He counted fifteen window-rattling thuds before a ghostly quiet fell, broken only by the barking of dogs. There were no sirens, no sound of police cars. He retired to bed.

The saboteurs had done well in Nicosia. Markos Drakos, head of the group which attacked the government radio station, planted his bombs in the main transformer house, while his guerrillas bound and gagged the watchmen. A hole was blown in the wall. The building caught fire and the roof caved in.

Other Nicosia groups threw fire bombs through the windows of government offices at the Secretariat, and at two army radio installations. It was all very amateurish: the Secretariat's attackers, for instance,

. . . drove up in an old Morris that broke down when we were a few hundred yards away. Someone got out to look under the bonnet and a grenade fell out of his satchel and bounced in the road. Quite a few bombs didn't go off, and the ones that did caused more smoke than fire. We drove away without seeing a soul. Afterwards, one of our group, Charalambos Xenofontos, picked up the EOKA leaflets from Drakos' house and distributed them in the street from his bicycle.[10]

But if the guerrillas were novices, the police were quite as raw. The colonial secretary (chief administrator of the island under the governor) and senior officers hurried to police headquarters, where all was confusion. Thirty constables paraded at two in the morning, then were sent to sit in the police canteen until dawn, while their superiors inspected the damage. At the Cyprus Broadcasting Service, one transmitter had survived, and a somewhat disjointed radio program went out next day. Pieces of Spey Royal whisky bottles, used to make Molotov cocktails, were gathered from the shattered machinery.

Grivas found the press a faster and more reliable source of information that morning than was his own organization. An aide brought the daily newspapers to his house on the Kyrenia road. The results seemed fairly satisfactory: the press estimated damage to CBS at more than one hundred and fifty thousand dollars. Lesser successes had been scored at the Secretariat and the army barracks. But outside Nicosia, EOKA was in trouble.

The Famagusta groups had failed in all their assaults on army depots and petrol dumps; a car loaded with bombs and EOKA leaflets had been captured and traced to Afxentiou, who was hiding in the fields near Lyssi, his home town. His rooms had been searched and orders from "Dighenis" discovered. Even the youth sent to cut the power lines had electrocuted himself.

At Larnaca the courthouse, police station, and administration offices had been damaged by bombs; but Poskottis and his group had been arrested.

Worst of all was the Limassol fiasco: Notis Petropouleas had arrived late and the attack had not begun until two in the morning, when the police had been alerted by telephone about raids in other towns. The guerrillas had flung their bombs too soon and fled. Three targets had been successfully attacked—two small police stations and a power plant; but a section leader, with all his men, had been caught. Petrol bombs, dropped in the night's confusion, were found by police outside the house containing the entire Limassol arsenal. It was searched, and hundreds of pounds of hard-won dynamite and TNT, old mines, and shells were seized.

The British made outraged protests at the attacks. The *Cyprus Mail* editorialized:

> Views on what should be done by Government differ only on the severity of the measures to be expected . . . all are agreed that acts of terrorism will never drive the British out of Cyprus—and that there is evidently a great deal of truth in Dr. Johnson's dictum that patriotism is the last refuge of a scoundrel.[11]

The governor, Sir Robert Armitage, said he was sure all law-abiding Cypriots shared his dismay at the attacks. But the popular Cypriot mood was compounded rather of shock and wonderment. Only the Communists openly disapproved, the local politbureau denouncing the bombings as "harmful to the struggle."

Grivas ordered attacks to continue on ensuing nights. A succession of bombs was thrown, mainly at the homes of British military men. A young hotel worker—sworn into EOKA by Droushiotis only twenty-four hours previously—was given an old Italian "red devil" grenade to hurl at the car of Sir Robert Armitage, as he left a Rotary dinner at the Ledra Palace Hotel on April 2; he dropped it from the roof as the car moved off at midnight. It missed by some yards, blowing a small crater in the driveway. No one was hurt.

For the next ten nights, attacks continued while Grivas sent out a stream of orders and letters. New leaders had to be found, more recruits sworn in. Athens Radio had to be scourged for its unhelpful attitude. The "Voice of the Fatherland" program—a propaganda commentary beamed at Cyprus—not only failed to praise the efforts of the fighters; it delivered a partisan eulogy of Socrates Loizides, who had sat for months in a Cyprus jail ever since the night of the capture of the ill-fated *St. George*. Grivas raged against "shameful exploitation of the work of others." When the tone of the broadcasts failed to improve, he wrote to Makarios:

> Today's broadcast was worse than yesterday's: it went so far as to say that freedom is not gained with terrorism, as Gandhi did not succeed in liberating India with means like this! Those who listened were petrified and asked themselves whether they should continue the struggle.[12]

The Archbishop replied on April 3 that the broadcasts had grieved him deeply; he would complain to Athens. Meanwhile, wrote Makarios:

> . . . you will certainly carry on the struggle with courage and confidence without being affected—although it is natural for you to be sorry—by acts of meanness which are completely temporary and will be surmounted soon.
>
> I am sending you my warmest wishes and sincere congratulations. One thousand bravos to you! The rulers have realized that we have entered upon a serious stage of struggle.[13]

This was the sugar coating on the pill that Makarios was about to administer: he wrote again within twenty-four hours to say that attacks should be halted while EOKA reorganized. Grivas was indignant: he felt that Makarios was surrounded by "faint-hearted" advisers who were "afraid for their skins." But the Archbishop's view prevailed, and by April 10 all EOKA action had ceased.

Grivas was disappointed by the reaction in Greece. A demonstration in favor of Enosis had been dispersed by the police, and there seemed to be no enthusiasm in the mother country for the revolution. "Nothing can be expected from them," wrote Grivas. "What can we do? We shall go on alone: but I am certain that when praises are awarded after the end of our struggle, we shall be given the crumbs whilst others will claim the victory." [14]

But there was consolation in the "great headache" they had given England, where Anthony Eden had replaced the aging Churchill as prime minister, and a new hand, Harold Macmillan, was at the helm in the Foreign Office. Both the Greek and Cypriot press were prophesying a change in British attitudes.

— 5 —

Riots, Bombings, and Attacks

After his failure in the Limassol attacks, Notis Petropouleas had reappeared in Nicosia. Grivas suspected him of treachery. It seemed that cowardice had been added to his known weaknesses for money and women; and—since he knew Grivas' hideouts—he was a menace to the whole organization. When Grivas heard that he had been picked up by the police he speedily moved to a safer residence, chosen by his brother Michael. This was the home of a cousin of the Grivas family, who lived in a quiet suburb a few hundred yards from the gates of Government House. A rear bedroom was prepared.

In all the years Grivas spent hiding in suburban homes, his routine scarcely varied. He rose at six in the morning and exercised for half an hour, either by walking in some sheltered back yard or with indoor calisthenics. Then he read every newspaper published in Cyprus and most of those from Greece. The rest of the day he devoted to writing and thinking: from his pen flowed an endless stream of instructions, memoranda, plans, and letters; the captured portion of his diary alone runs to some quarter-million words, and it is perhaps not so much as a third of the whole. In the early days, Grivas received several couriers daily with messages from the district leaders; later on, for security reasons, he reduced the number to a minimum. After dark, whenever possible, he took exercise. Sometimes he walked at a brisk pace along Churchill Avenue—a quiet area where he would encounter few pedestrians—as far as the gates of Government House.

Grivas considered having Notis Petropouleas killed; he was unreliable and already the British were offering cash rewards for information. But

Notis, whatever his failings, was liked by many in the organization and they obtained a false passport for him through contacts in the civil service and he left for Beirut.

Grivas at this time returned to his main headquarters on the Kyrenia road and took up one of his lifetime preoccupations, the Communist menace. It was, for him, real enough: soon after April 1 the exiled head of the rebel Communist movement in Greece, Nikos Zachariades, had revealed the identity of "Dighenis" in a broadcast from behind the Iron Curtain, whence he had fled after the defeat of Communist forces in the forties. Underground Communists in Athens had obtained the information through a member of an early "liberation committee."

Grivas now set his own spies to watch the Cypriot Communists and warned them in a leaflet that any action on their part against EOKA would be punished. He also urged Makarios to see that "the authorities in Athens should not grant visas for Cyprus to Communists in Greece." This concern with the Communist party was not shared by the Archbishop, although he was aware of its potentialities.

Not least among Grivas' annoyances was the timid attitude of the Cypriot press toward their struggle. Why, for example, had no newspaper protested against the night curfews the authorities were trying to impose on young people? The press, Grivas raged, "are interested only in their pockets," and he urged Makarios to put some ginger into the editors.

Polycarpos Georgadjis' intelligence network now included half a dozen policemen, who were supplying EOKA with information on police arms stores, weapon strength, plans, and projects. These "EOKA policemen" at first handed their information to student runners, but after one of them was almost caught while carrying a written report to Georgadjis, the intelligence chief arranged for them to pass news on verbally through older and more reliable contacts; sometimes he himself met the policemen, in cafes and restaurants. By the end of June 1955, Georgadjis had increased the number of policemen helping the organization to twenty, from all branches of the force.

EOKA was now manufacturing its own grenades: they consisted of a water pipe junction fitted with a heavy base plate and a screw cap, filled with sharp metal fragments and the explosive charge; the fuse protruded through the cap, and could be lit with a cigarette end. These pipe bombs were manufactured by the score at the workshop of Stylianos Lenas, a Nicosia plumber, and in the basement of Nicosia's leading hotel, the

Ledra Palace, where the handyman Yannakis Pafitis, an EOKA member, had a workroom.

By the end of May, Grivas was ready for the second phase of action. He sent a report [1] on his achievements and plans to the Archbishop:

> The struggle must be organised in such a way that it will last *at least* until next October, when the Cyprus question will be discussed in the UNO.
>
> This plan will be executed *in stages*. On the one hand we shall disperse, fatigue and irritate the enemy and on the other hand we shall see how we can reach the final stage of the plan without running the risk of seeing our struggle suppressed prematurely, before October.

So:

> At the beginning we shall organize acts of sabotage in the towns and in important communication centers, with simultaneous attacks on police stations especially in the mountain areas, in order to compel the enemy to disperse his forces.
>
> Then we shall go on with activity by small groups of armed men in mountainous areas which will make sudden attacks and then hide themselves. The targets will be police station and Army camps.
>
> Finally, if the above are crowned with success, we shall organize a general uprising of the youth in the towns and the country with militant demonstrations. The organized population will also participate. These militant demonstrations are being organized by us.

Grivas concluded that the plan could be modified to meet the needs of Makarios' diplomatic strategy. The one thing that could not be altered was a continued armed struggle "because its abandonment will mean the interment of the Enosis question." Once again, Grivas feared the Archbishop might listen to those in Athens who were crying "enough."

Grivas now gave orders for major student demonstrations. May 24 was Empire Day, when schools and public offices closed. Nearly one thousand young students stoned administration buildings and pulled down a Union Jack. Grivas ordered that they should not disperse when the police arrived, but retaliate. This they did with a will.

Crowds of young people swept through the streets, chanting in unison ENOSIS, EOKA, and MAKARIOS. The voices echoed across the city like the roar of the sea, punctuated by the crash of glass as a window went, or a hail of bottles—brought up to the rear by schoolgirls—rained down on the Cypriot police. Outnumbered and outmaneuvered, the police called in the army. But by the time troops arrived the demonstration was drawing to a close, as planned, outside the Archbishop's palace.

For the British, it posed a new problem. They faced a manpower shortage and the inexperienced army draftees, little older than the Cypriot students, had no training in mob control. The local English-language *Cyprus Mail* suggested spraying offenders with chemical dyes, or using a method its editor recalled from Indian days, by which "demonstrators are bundled into police vans, driven twenty miles out into the desert, have their shoes taken from them and are told to walk home."

That day the press also carried the news that the governor, Sir Robert Armitage, would attend the premiere of a British film in aid of British Legion funds, as part of the Empire Day celebrations. Reading this, Markos Drakos conceived the idea of planting a bomb beneath the governor's chair. Some hours before the governor's arrival an EOKA man entered the theater and planted the bomb in the flag-draped balcony. Unsure where Sir Robert Armitage would sit, he chose a spot near the front and left just as police entered for a search.

They failed to find the bomb. But the film, "Forbidden Cargo," ended sooner than expected and the governor's party departed five minutes before the bomb exploded, six rows from where he had been sitting with the colonial secretary, the chief justice and their wives. Their escape was a narrow one. Two rows of seats were shattered by the blast, a hole was blown in the floor, and the ceiling peppered with flying debris.

The Archbishop approved of the youth activities, but Grivas had the impression that he planned to keep firm control over them. He wrote later in his diary:

> He asked me about the arms we need. It is only now that he has understood that we need arms as well!! Oh! If only I had the brains before which I have now!! No one wanted to listen to me when we had the chance. Now he wants them!
>
> He wants us to start. Papagos asked him why he stopped!! Another one who wants everything ready for exploitation! I told him that I shall start after the end of the old moon. We parted with his blessings: good success.[2]

As a prelude to the new island-wide attack, the Archbishop for the first time obliquely endorsed EOKA, publicly praising the "admirable militancy" of the people and charging the British with unleashing "terror and repression."

Before action began, Grivas drove to the mountains to meet Renos Kyriakides, younger brother of the bishop of Kyrenia, who was forming the first mountain guerrilla band. They discussed the possibility of ambushing trucks carrying explosives to the mines at Amiandos, and Grivas gave instructions for attacks against village police stations. They lunched together under the pines at the monastery of Mesapotamos before Grivas returned to the capital. On the way back, the police waved them to a halt. Grivas and his bodyguard kept their hands on their pistols as a sergeant leaned in to ask if they would take a villager, wounded in a tavern fight, to a hospital.

On the night of June 19, 1955, a flurry of bombs exploded in every major town. The targets ranged from bars frequented by troops, to the homes of British officers, to police stations, army canteens, and barracks. A time bomb dropped into a letter box at the entrance to Nicosia Central Police Station exploded while the street was crowded with shoppers, killing a Greek Cypriot and wounding a dozen Turks and Armenians. The bomb was the most powerful yet used: it blew a large hole in a wall of divisional police headquarters.

Another bomb, carried into Famagusta police headquarters by a Cypriot constable, was taped to the inside of a chimney. It blew the roof off. The homes of a local army commander and of a high-ranking political adviser to Middle East HQ were hit by hand grenades; in the latter case, the grenade was thrown by the adviser's own Cypriot chauffeur. A raid on Amiandos police station went well. Kyriakides' group riddled the building with gunfire, killing a sergeant and wounding a constable, then stripped the armory of rifles and shotguns.

Grivas was pleased with the first results. But as the nights passed and military patrols began to stop all cars on the main roads to hunt for arms, the explosions lessened. He summed up the second burst of violence in an order to all district leaders:

> The material results were lower than I expected. Each district leader is to summon his group leaders and they must make a self-criticism together to discover the mistakes that have been made and ensure they are not repeated.[3]

However, he added, EOKA had shown the world that the rigid British policy of "never" to self-determination could be shaken. Now they must prepare for another round of action to meet the new Greek appeal on the question of Cyprus to the U.N.

The object of our next operations will be to terrorize the police and to paralyze the administration both inside cities and in the country. If this object is attained, the results will be as follows:

Disillusion of the police with the prevailing state of affairs so that, most probably, if they do not help us openly, they will tolerate our actions.

Active intervention of the Army in security, a thing which will deploy and tire them out. This will react on the Army's morale and also influence its leaders.

In the face of our strength and persistence and the trouble caused, it is very probable that the United Nations and even interested members of NATO, will seek an understanding.

The desired results, he went on, would be obtained by:

1. Murderous attacks against policemen who are out of sympathy with our aims or who try to hunt us down.
2. Ambushes against police patrols in towns, or raids on country police stations.
3. Obstructing free movement of the police across the island by laying ambushes (against individuals or groups).[4]

Above all, more "traitors" must be executed. But it was not easy to persuade the mild and law-abiding Cypriots to eliminate people on mere suspicion. Grivas had frequent cause to rail against the "faint-heartedness" of his would-be gunmen.

Collision with Britain

It was the Cypriots' misfortune that the start of their revolution should coincide with the brief but calamitous rule of Sir Anthony Eden, whose policies in the Middle East favored, for several reasons, the Turks. In his global strategy Cyprus was a pawn: his generals assured him it was vital to the maintenance of Britain's position in the Middle East, to her oil interests in the Persian Gulf, and to her control over the Suez Canal. Eden had also to consider the wishes of U.S. Secretary of State John Foster Dulles, who sought an alliance of Middle Eastern countries to "contain" Russia and halt the spread of Communist influence, already apparent in President Nasser's Egypt. Turkey was of the greatest importance to both British and American designs for the Middle East, and in the Baghdad Pact—an alliance of Britain, Turkey, Iraq, Iran, and Pakistan, engineered by Eden and signed only a few days before the start of EOKA action—the Turks were the vital partners.

As he was to remark later in his memoirs, the British premier "regarded our alliance with the Turks as the first consideration in our policy in that part of the world." [1] For this the Turks exacted a high price from both Britain and the United States in political concessions and financial aid.

For all its anxiety to preserve the status quo in Cyprus, the British government—harassed by the Labour party and left-wing press at home, and by newly liberated colonial countries behind the scenes at the U.N.—felt obliged to take some political initiative. "Never" was a word that could never again be used by a minister of the crown with regard to the island's claim to self-determination. So much EOKA had achieved. On June 30, 1955, therefore, Sir Anthony Eden announced that Greek and Turkish representatives had been invited to a conference on "questions concerning the Eastern Mediterranean, including Cyprus." No Cypriots were invited, but the colonial secretary, Alan Lennox-Boyd, flew to the island and offered the Archbishop a new constitution, with no prospect of self-determination in the foreseeable future. Makarios reaffirmed his stand on self-determination and objected to the invitation to Turkey, which gave that country its first official recognition as an equal partner in the dispute.

At the same time, Britain began to build up her security forces in Cyprus, and dispatched the chief of the imperial general staff, Field Marshal Sir John Harding, to examine the military situation. The police would be re-equipped, their ranks increased with Turkish Cypriot volunteers and with British experts imported from similar trouble spots within the Empire. A mobile reserve and other specialized groups of a paramilitary nature were planned to counter EOKA. Laws were introduced which made possible the detention of Cypriots without trial. The first detention center was created behind the stout walls of Kyrenia Castle, built at the start of the Latin occupation in the twelfth century.

Grivas, meanwhile, was plotting the murder of Police Superintendent Kyriakos Aristotelous, whom EOKA regarded as the most dangerous man in the force. Keenly pro-British, yet admired for fairness and honesty in the community, he was behind most of the successful blows struck against the organization, and his loyal following in the police constituted a "private army."

"Kyriacoudi"—as Cypriots called him—had planted informers inside the organization in Nicosia. The names and homes of its leaders were known to him, and he was paying well for further information. To a student who had revealed the names of youths in his group he had paid two hundred pounds (approximately five hundred dollars),[2] and many times that sum was offered for information about "Dighenis" himself.

Early in July, Aristotelous descended on the houses used by EOKA in the capital and arrested Evangelakis, the city leader, his aide Markos Drakos, and half a dozen other key figures. After lengthy interrogation, these men were sent to the Kyrenia Castle detention center.

In one night, this well-planned raid disrupted months of training and organization. Not knowing where the next blow might fall, Grivas left his house on the Kyrenia road and returned to Strovolos, the suburb near Government House, to the home of Stelios Kyranides, a friendly clerk in the Government Land Registry Office. Although occupied much of the day with writing and organizational work, Grivas discovered that Kyranides was a stamp collector. A keen philatelist himself, Grivas turned out a drawer of stamps and spent several hours sorting and sticking them in an album. Droushiotis, the courier, raised an eyebrow at this spectacle; but Grivas was not deterred from his solitary addiction.

This respite was short-lived. A few days after Grivas moved police began searches in Strovolos. "Kyriacoudi" was at work again. Grivas decided the capital was getting too hot for him, and it was time, in any case, to take over in person the training of the mountain guerrillas.

On July 5, 1955, he was driven in Pascalis Papadopoulos' car to the Troodos mountains, where Renos Kyriakides waited. In one of his pockets was the revolver he had used since World War I; in the other a grenade. It would be nearly four years before he saw Nicosia again. Once more, glass jars containing his precious diaries were given to Pascalis Papadopoulos for burial in the earth.

A letter from the Archbishop followed Grivas. Makarios, struck by the fact that a colonial secretary whose predecessors had for years refused to receive delegations from Cyprus should now come running to the island for talks, told Grivas on July 12:

> EOKA has contributed infinitely more to the Cyprus struggle than 75 years of paper warfare. The name Dighenis is an enigma to the British and at the same time a legend. It has already passed into the pages of the history of liberation movements.[3]

Bombs had been exploded in government buildings during the Makarios–Lennox-Boyd discussions to suggest, as it were, the unofficial presence of EOKA at any negotiations. One of these had been planted, in the office where he worked, by Michael Caraolis, a young civil servant, who was to become famous as the first of many young gunmen to be hanged by the British.

Georgadjis was organizing "execution squads" to carry out the threat contained in EOKA's latest leaflet:

> TO THE POLICE: I have warned you: you have taken this warning as a mere threat, and my forbearance has weakened. What I have threatened I will carry out to the letter. . . . Do not try to block our path or you will stain it with your blood. But you will not stop us. . . .
> I have given instructions:
> Anyone who tries to stop the Cypriot patriots will be EXECUTED.

YOU HAVE NOTHING TO FEAR SO LONG AS YOU DO NOT
GET IN OUR WAY.[4]

The boys whom Georgadjis chose for his first killer squad were in no
sense "street people": they came from middle-class backgrounds, had
attended the island's best schools and were destined to rise in their
chosen careers: one was a law student, two were graduates of the English School—a British-run college—a fourth was a medical student.
The fifth was Michael Caraolis. All were volunteers from EOKA sabotage or intelligence groups.

Their first target was Police Constable Herodotus Poullis, a member
of "Kyriacoudi's" private army who had already escaped one attack.
Caraolis and the others had stalked Poullis for some time. On August 28
Poullis and a Turkish Cypriot policeman were keeping a plainclothes
watch on a leftist political meeting. About a thousand members of the
left-wing trade union had gathered to hear the secretary of the local
Communist party, AKEL, denounce the coming three-power conference
in London as "a British trap," and take a dig at the church-sponsored
EOKA. Communist leaders had received threatening letters, said the
secretary, Ezekial Papaioannou, but they had treated them with con-
tempt. "We do not know and do not wish to learn the cowardly tactics
of political murder."

As the crowd emerged into the street, Caraolis strode toward his victim and shot him three times in the chest. The gunman and his ac-
complices fled on foot, escaping pursuit in the maze of narrow side
streets. But six days later, as Caraolis was being driven to join the
Kyrenia mountain guerrillas, he was picked up by police. Three Turkish
witnesses identified him as the killer. Further assassinations of policemen that month started a wave of resignations and secret defections to
EOKA within the force.

Day after day, "Cypriot patriots" were urged by Athens Radio to
greater deeds of "daring," and the police enjoined to "save themselves
from death's embrace" by joining EOKA. "The punishment of the de-
testable special constable," said the radio after one killing, "is severe
but just. He agreed to betray his country for the sake of a few pounds.
Let this be a lesson to those who forget their most holy duty." [5]

No attempt was made to jam the broadcasts, or to censor the blood-
thirsty editorializing of the Athenian press, which was freely obtainable

in the island. But the British did begin to mount a propaganda counterattack in broadcasts over their CBS that set the tone of official statements for the next few years. Acting colonial secretary, H. Sykes, denounced "callous and cowardly murderers" who were the "evil agents of political terrorism." Everything possible, he said, would be done to preserve law and order.[6] To prove his words, the first mass search operations began in town and country.

The police scored a notable success with the arrest of Polycarpos Georgadjis and two youths belonging to his execution squads. The three had gone to reconnoiter the home of a police inspector when they were stopped and searched. The youths were later jailed for carrying arms; but Georgadjis, whose pockets contained only a list of Turkish witnesses to the Caraolis shooting, could not be brought to trial. He was sent to join the other EOKA prisoners in Kyrenia Castle.

Now every Greek Cypriot might expect at any moment to be bodily searched as he walked the streets or drove about. Not even the person of the Archbishop was sacrosanct. One Saturday evening, on his way to dedicate a church at Lefkonico, Makarios' caravan of cars was halted by an army patrol. Makarios was ordered to descend from his car while suitcases containing his ceremonial vestments were searched and the following carloads of priests and ethnarchy officials minutely examined. In a sermon the next day, Makarios declared that he would never again submit to such indignity:

> This is the life of slaves, filled with humiliation. What did they hope to discover? It is mainly with the weapons of the soul that we are struggling. . . .[7]

Before the three-power conference on Cyprus began, he drove to the mountains for a meeting—the last for almost four years—with Grivas, who had been moving among the villages of the Troodos range since early July, staying with the guerrillas and seeking sites for the ambush of army trucks. In that rugged country, heavily wooded and crisscrossed by paths negotiable only on foot, the opportunities were many, and isolated supply vehicles were frequent.

On the night of July 30, Grivas was asleep in Kyperounda when a patrol arrived. He ordered his men up and out of the village. Guns were wrapped in sacking and loaded on mules. At first light the group made for the hills, Grivas bringing up the rear with a Greek Cypriot woman whose presence allayed military suspicions. They passed within a few hundred yards of three truckloads of troops, who took them for peasants off to the fields.

In the mountains, Grivas changed his appearance to suit his surroundings; whereas in town he had been a sober-suited citizen with dark glasses and homburg, here he became the typical Cypriot peasant, darkening his pale, townsman's face with olive oil to encourage his tan, even occasionally adopting a pair of *vrachi*—the baggy black peasant trousers. He allowed his military moustache to develop into something more flowing and patriarchal. He felt healthier and in higher spirits than at any time since his arrival.[8]

The guerrilla groups were awaiting his word to start action in the mountains, but now the London talks were under way, and Makarios could not appreciate the glories of the campaign Grivas had projected. There was scope yet for action in the towns; he saw no immediate need for an offensive elsewhere. Grivas wrote in his diary:

> . . . is he afraid of losses? Or of responsibility for bloodshed? Perhaps it is a matter of pride because he spoke against guerrilla action from the start and did not want to bring in the necessary arms.[9]

The Archbishop used the occasion of religious festival at Trooditissa monastery to cover his meeting with Grivas. After one of his most belligerent speeches yet, to a holiday crowd of some ten thousand souls ("slavery can no longer be tolerated . . . the British grant freedom only to those who are determined to take it"), Makarios drove to the OXEN summer youth camp near Kakopetria. Grivas had arrived before dawn and was waiting in a tent under the pines on the edge of the clearing. Makarios sat knee to knee with the EOKA leader for nearly an hour exchanging news.

Grivas recounted his plans for the next round and Makarios discussed their financing and the political progress made. He had little hope for the tripartite conference; and he would continue to urge the Greek government to concentrate its efforts on international pressure at the United Nations.

And indeed, the conference, held in London in September 1955, served only to divide still further the three disputants: the Turks claimed that if Britain should abdicate her rights to Cyprus, the island must revert to them; the Greeks pressed for self-determination—then a diplomatic term for Enosis; and the British presented a plan for "limited self-government," with no change in their sovereignty over the island "in the foreseeable future." Greece was told that "we do not accept the principle of self-determination as one of universal application." [10]

On the day this plan was revealed, the Greek minorities of Istanbul and Izmir were subjected to a pogrom of extraordinary violence in which millions of dollars worth of damage was done to Greek property: churches were burned down, stores looted, even graveyards assailed and coffins exhumed and their contents thrown into the street. Not only Greeks, but Armenians and Jews were killed; and only when Turkish Prime Minister Adnan Menderes called out the army was order restored. Menderes was later charged by his own countrymen with responsibility for the pogrom, which began following a bomb explosion at the Turkish consulate in Salonika. It seems that he had planned the demonstration to emphasize Turkey's interest in Cyprus.

The effect of the conference, then, was to place Turkey in the fore-front of the political picture and present Britain as mediator in a dispute between two rival claimants. This role proved useful when, on September 21, the Greek appeal on Cyprus was presented at the United Nations. After Greece had rejected strong American pressure to drop her plea, its inscription on the U.N. General Assembly's agenda was rejected by the steering committee. While riots and strikes pursued their familiar course in Cyprus, the Athenian press accused the United States of blackmail and bribery.

Dulles, like Eden, was not anxious to offend Turkey, whose frontiers were sown with American missiles. Acceptance of the Turkish position on Cyprus meant, in Eden's words, that "Enosis must be ruled out as a solution." [11] In return for this use of Turkish soil as a base and Turkish intransigence as a lever, Menderes sought aid totaling three hundred and fifty million dollars from the United States to finance his bankrupt regime.

The contretemps at the U.N. did at least clarify the attitudes of the participants: while Turkey balanced her strategical interest in Cyprus against the need for dollars, the U.S. State Department would try to maintain the appearance of impartiality; and the British could turn their attentions to restoring law and order in Cyprus, which meant a vigorous campaign to destroy EOKA.

Three days after the United Nations rejected discussion of Cyprus, it was announced that Sir Robert Armitage would be replaced as governor by the retiring chief of the imperial staff, Sir John Harding.

Harding Takes Charge

If any doubts remained in London about the need for a military man in Cyprus, they were dispelled that month. First the British Council—a bastion of Anglo-Cypriot culture and friendship—was burned to the ground by a mob. Next, sixteen of the most important EOKA members, so painstakingly gathered up by police over the months, escaped in a night from Kyrenia Castle. Most of them joined Grivas and his mountain guerrillas.

Throughout the summer of 1955, thousands of sticks of dynamite were taken from the mines, and the armories of rural police stations were stripped of their guns. But it was not enough. Grivas bombarded his associates in Athens with demands for arms. He needed time pencils, high explosives, and portable automatic weapons—none of which were available in Cyprus. Grivas said that these supplies could be obtained from Greek army stores. This the Athens conspirators knew; what they did not know was how to get them to Cyprus.

A slightly comic episode had occurred back in July, when an EOKA agent flew to Athens to pick up a parcel of explosives and time pencils. He returned to Limassol by ship, dropped the waterproofed package over the side in shallow water with a cork marker attached, and returned the next day in a small boat to collect it. But the depth of the harbor at that point was more than one hundred feet, and he spent a frustrating day circling the waters in a hired boat—the string attached to the cork marker was too short.

EOKA, however, had recruited several Greek-Cypriot customs officials; and with their help a flow of arms was brought in through the port of Limassol. Security—considering that an armed revolt had been

under way for several months—was incredibly lax. One British collector
of customs with a handful of policemen presided over a team of Cypriot
examiners who did all the work. The Athens group were told to pack
two stout suitcases with guns and explosives, give them to a courier,
and leave the rest to EOKA. Two Cypriot students then studying theology at Athens University were selected for the mission.

The first was Patroclus Stavrou, a protege of Makarios, whose private
secretary he later became. The second was Maroulla Papamiltiades,—
the prefix "papa" to her name indicated that her father was a priest—
whose family was related to the Archbishop. It was she who helped
pack the suitcases with an assortment of pistols, machine guns, TNT,
and time pencils. Colored string was tied to the suitcase handles to identify them to customs men in EOKA. A dab of chalk, and the cases
passed through unchecked and were hustled out to the street where a
car was waiting to drive them to Nicosia. The arms were unpacked in an
annex of the Archbishop's palace.

A key to the operation, which was repeated many times in ensuing
months, was that the suitcases at any given moment on board or in the
customs shed, were under supervision—yet ownerless. Before the
EOKA smuggler sailed for Cyprus, detailed written instructions told the
customs men what to expect. They knew the ship bringing the arms;
they knew the cases, by description and certain prearranged markings—
three blue suitcases, for example, marked boldly in red with the letters
AL and with a strip of Speedfix around the edge. All the smuggler had
to do was see that the cases were among the last to leave the ship, so
that baggage could pile up in the customs shed and make it easier, in the
confusion of a Mediterranean arrival, for the officials to pass them
through unopened.

The smugglers in Greece found other, more bizarre, methods of ex-
porting arms to Cyprus. Selected Cypriot students were sent on holiday
trips to Athens, from which they returned with ash trays made of solid
explosive and painted with blue and white maps of Cyprus.

When Bishop Anthimos of Kitium visited Athens in October 1955,
his episcopal staff—a hollow metal rod made of sections which screwed
into one another, and topped with a brass eagle—was filled with eight
time pencils.

His traveling companion, Father Kallinikos, wore a black, cylindrical
priest's hat. Into the padded crown were sewn nine time pencils. The
two prelates were met on their return at the airport by the Archbishop's

personal secretary, Pascal Pascalides, who found Father Kallinikos nervously patting down his hat. But Bishop Anthimos, his weighted staff in one hand, embraced Pascalides calmly, and the party passed through a customs check without mishap.

On a later visit to Athens, Bishop Anthimos was presented with a teddy bear to take back to a Nicosia orphanage. Maroulla Papamiltiades had unraveled the seams and concealed in the stuffing a dozen time pencils. The bishop put the bear with other bric-a-brac purchased in the Greek capital and it passed safely through.

The smugglers grew increasingly daring. Late in 1955, they embarked on their most ambitious scheme so far—and ran into difficulties. Eight time pencils had been hidden in the bindings of a book and sent to Cyprus without the knowledge or consent of the Greek foreign ministry—in the diplomatic bag to the consulate in Cyprus. This success inspired the smugglers to pack the biggest consignment of arms yet assembled into cases of religious books destined for a Limassol bookstore. Four large crates were filled with nineteen limpet mines, fourteen grenades, four .38 pistols, two Thompson submachine guns, one Sten, TNT, and large quantities of ammunition. On top were laid Bibles, New Testaments, and a variety of devotional works. A fifth case contained only books, for it would be opened by EOKA's customs agent on arrival in Limassol.

But when the S.S. *Aeolia* docked, on the afternoon of December 3, it soon became clear that the smugglers had been betrayed. The police knew what they were looking for, and exactly where to find it. They waited until four in the morning of the next day before picking up the consignee, a Limassol bookseller, in the hope that other members of EOKA would visit him and fall into the net.

It was a blow for EOKA: not the loss of the arms so much as the tightening of security that followed. The Greek-Cypriot customs officials fell under suspicion. Army intelligence officers and a detachment of soldiers were permanently installed at the customs depot. Later, customs experts were brought from Britain. Yet suitcases of arms continued to arrive from Athens by the old method for many months after the seizure of the *Aeolia*'s cargo.

Field Marshal Sir John Harding, arrived in Cyprus on October 3, 1955, to take up his final post as governor of the island. His career had brought him to the height of his profession. "No greater compliment," wrote Grivas later, "could have been paid us than to send against our

tiny forces a man with so great a reputation and so brilliant a career." [1]
On his heels came an array of famous British regiments—Gordon Highlanders, Royal Norfolks, the Middlesex Regiment, the commandos: by
mid-October there were twelve thousand troops in the island and soon
that number would be doubled. A legal expert from the Colonial Office
appeared to map out the needs of a "State of Emergency": special
courts, special justices, and a new set of draconic laws to deal with the
mass of EOKA offenders who would soon be choking the courts.

Harding spoke of "a spider's web" of security measures across the
island in which the terrorist flies would be caught: every student demonstration would be met with curfew; every ambush or attack with a search
operation. The upper echelons of the security forces were shaken out to
provide full and quick coordination. Hundreds of police constables were
brought from Britain, promoted to sergeant and given increased pay.
And hundreds of Turkish Cypriots were recruited for a riot-breaking
"mobile reserve," armed with guns, gas, and a variety of other equipment, including an improved model of what had been dubbed "the Armitage patent anti-Coca-Cola bottle shield." Army sentries with rifles
waited on rooftops to guard British shoppers; patrols increased everywhere; and over the police headquarters in Nicosia loomed a symbol of
this reorganization—a tall radio tower which would eventually link the
most outlying posts with the capital.

At Kakopetria, high in the mountains, Grivas watched these preparations unperturbed. The larger the army, the more cumbrous a weapon it
became to use against his invisible units. It is doubtful if EOKA contained at this time as many as five hundred sworn members—though
support for the organization among the people was growing from day to
day. Grivas was sure that he could make up for the disparity through
better use of the element of surprise. Britain's show of strength was intended to reinforce its position at the conference table, at which Harding
was soon to sit with Makarios and bargain on the basis of granting "a
wide measure of self-government." The two men met within the first
week of Harding's assumption of political and military control.

Makarios thought Harding more straightforward than were the politicians in London. Grivas, too, regarded him with greater deference than
other British commanders who later tried their hand in Cyprus. But
Harding, he says, "seriously underestimated an opponent whom he took
to be a few undisciplined bands of hotheads which could easily be
broken up." [2]

Grivas criticized the Harding strategy on three grounds: first, there were "theatrical military movements such as Cyprus had never seen before." These, he conceded, were tactically logical, but frustrated in practice by the clumsiness of the troops on the ground. Second, the security forces, wittingly or not, terrorized the population and aided Grivas' plan "to turn the whole island into a field of battle so that the enemy should not feel secure anywhere." And third, the British "launched a silly propaganda campaign against us" which, in its denigration of the Cyprus Church and other institutions, offended even the more moderate Cypriots.[3]

An example of how Grivas was able to make use of British efforts to dampen nationalistic ardor is offered by "the Battle of the Flags." Everywhere in the island, for decades, it had been the custom of Greek Cypriots to fly over schools the blue and white flag of Greece. Now this "foreign flag" was deemed a provocation and when schools persisted in flying it, troops were sent, time and time again, to haul it down.

Grivas saw that here even the primary schools could play a role. Pupils were told to hoist the flag deliberately on school buildings while British troops patrolled the villages. Then, to the jeers and laughter of children, a sweating serviceman would scramble up the flagpole, while fellow soldiers with guns stood guard. It was not calculated to inspire respect for the forces of law and order, and it took from operational duties men who would have been better employed elsewhere. Later, flagpoles were mined and soldiers killed or maimed.

Youth demonstrations were EOKA's preferred weapon while the early talks between Makarios and Harding progressed. The worst came at Famagusta where some four thousand people marched the streets cheering for Enosis. Troops were stoned and they retaliated by spraying the rioters with green dye from curious, tire-shaped containers strapped to their backs. Across the island there were thousands of arrests, broken windows, and broken heads. Soldiers were wounded by bombs thrown in the melee. As the chaos reached its height it was announced that Caraolis had been sentenced to death: he would be the first EOKA youth to hang.

Makarios had ordered that there should be no EOKA attacks during this early phase of his negotiations with Harding, but small-scale raids and shootings went on sporadically. Grivas wanted to keep up the fighting morale not only of his organization but of the general public. Guerrillas at Famagusta raided a military store at the docks. A vital lock was smashed during the day by a crane operator. The EOKA men had only to walk in and overpower a watchman. They piled cases of arms, freshly arrived from Suez, onto their lorry and made off with a dozen machine guns, six mortars, and four bazookas.

In November, Harding returned to London for consultations on the progress of his discussions. The Archbishop flew to Athens for talks with the new government of Constantine Karamanlis; Papagos had died on October 5. As 1956 approached attitudes hardened and Grivas began to plan a new campaign of sabotage and assassination.

— 8 —

The Mountain Guerrillas

Grivas spent the last months of 1955 moving from village to village in the mountains, organizing and training the first guerrilla groups. His weapons were few, his men tough, eager, and wholly inexperienced. Reno Kyriakides had formed a few nuclei in the area. They lived by day in the houses of EOKA members and village priests; by night they went out into the forests with pick and shovel to hack holes in which caches of arms and explosives could be hidden. Oil drums were placed in each hole and packed with weapons and bombs.

Work began on a series of underground hideouts which would serve as Grivas' headquarters. Military patrols were becoming more frequent in the mountains; more than once Grivas had found himself cooped up in a village house, obliged to watch from an upstairs window while soldiers lounged and drank outside the neighboring cafe.

The site chosen for the mountain headquarters was a massive height in the vast Adelphi forest. From the topmost ridge the view was magnificent. Hill upon hill rolled away, the slopes shrouded in pine and fir. Among bushes and boulders, Kyriakides' men hacked out seven caves, each capable of holding four to five men. Sheets of corrugated iron were brought up from the villages by donkey-back to roof the holes, while the entrances were shrouded with undergrowth. Each hideout was entered through an opening barely wide enough for a man's body and sealed from inside by a wooden trap. The guerrillas dubbed this eyrie ''the Castle.''

Grivas had issued orders and assigned targets for the next phase of the attack, which he named ''Operation Forward to Victory.'' It would commence on November 18, the day on which Archbishop Makarios was due to return from talks in Athens with the Greek government.

Grivas decided to set an example by leading one ambush himself. Before dawn on November 23 he took fifteen men to a sharp bend in a lonely mountain road that led from Kyperounda to Agros. Renos Kyriakides loaded a donkey with land mines to plant in the road along which military vehicles made a daily supply run. By first light Grivas had concealed his men, in three groups, around the site. It was bitterly cold. The year's first snow had fallen during the night.

At three in the afternoon a British armored scout car and a Land-Rover approached. One of Grivas' men waved a signal flag and another opened fire without waiting for Grivas' order. The antiquated land mines failed to explode and the scout car made off toward Agros. But grenades hit the Land-Rover and in a cross-fire of bullets, it plunged over the edge of a ravine, killing its two occupants.

The guerrillas withdrew to the heights and watched through binoculars as, some two hours later, a rescue party scrambled three hundred feet down the mountainside to the wreck. That night they traveled back to their base at "the Castle," taking six hours to cover the seven-mile distance. Sometimes in the blackness they lost the forest track as it fell into deep valleys then rose to cross razor-backed ridges two thousand feet high. An icy rain fell continuously.

At the same time the campaign went forward in all the main towns. During the first day of the operation more than fifty bombs exploded. An EOKA cell at work in the Nicosia Post Office planted a homemade device in the main letter box, bringing down a corner of the building. Targets ranged from bars frequented by the British to village police stations; weapons ranged from a bottle filled with petrol to a vegetable can packed with TNT. Among the dead was the first military victim of EOKA's "execution squads," an army sergeant, who was shot in the head and back by a youth on a bicycle who pedaled away unchecked by Cypriot witnesses.

Harding's reaction was to declare a state of emergency. Draconic new laws known euphemistically as "emergency regulations" permitted the whipping of boys under eighteen years of age; the execution of men and women for illegal possession of firearms or explosives; life imprisonment for acts of sabotage; the deportation of political prisoners and local leaders suspected of "endangering public safety," and much more of the same stamp. The governor was empowered to seize newspapers, close them down and prosecute their editors for causing "alarm and despondency." Powers of search without warrant were granted to the police and freely practiced by the military; strikes and public meetings were declared illegal. The power of detention without trial was expanded to include virtually anyone upon whom suspicion fell; and property could be seized at the briefest notice. Almost immediately, prominent Cypriots by the score were arrested and packed off to a detention camp, known as Camp K, among them the seven directors of one of the largest firms on the island and a leading Nicosia gynecologist, who was taken from his clinic moments after completing an operation.

Since the end of World War II, a series of rebellions in British colonies from Malaya to Kenya had established a routine of repression (Harding himself was credited with crushing the uprising in East Africa), and this was now applied to Cyprus. The population was fingerprinted and issued identity cards; collective fines were levied on villages and towns where "outrages" occurred; tracts of the island were placed under curfew, by day or night, while house-to-house searches were made by the army, which took over all responsibility for security.

All this suited Grivas' purpose. The island was flooded with troops that offended the population and provided targets for EOKA's guns; and a civil policy was instituted which drove people into EOKA's arms.

On the day that Harding signed the proclamation of a state of emergency an attempt was made on his life. He was to attend, on the evening of November 26, an annual ball arranged by the Caledonian Society at the Ledra Palace Hotel. An odd-job man, Yannis Pafitis, who held the keys of a box containing the hotel's main power switches was given the task of planning and executing the attempt single-handed. He carried grenades into the building in a basket of oranges, and when the dancing was under way he cut the electric power. In the confusion that followed he hurled two grenades at the governor's table, but Harding had canceled his visit at the last moment. Several guests were hit by flying metal and water from a pierced radiator flooded the floor.

Pafitis ran to the basement and turned on the lights, then returned to the hall with blankets for the wounded. The Nicosia commissioner had him arrested along with the rest of the hotel staff. The local English-language newspaper described the scene:

> . . . . After the explosion, the Royal Scots band played *Glasgow Belongs to Me,* and everyone wanted to continue dancing but as the water on the floor made this impossible the assembled Britons, after singing *God Save the Queen* with fervour, adjourned to the refreshment bar. [1]

Pafitis was questioned by the police, but they did not suspect him, and he was released a few days later.

The tempo of "Operation Forward to Victory" was maintained throughout December. A grenade was hurled through the windows of the Cyprus Airways' office. A time bomb exploded in the office of Martin Clemens, the commissioner of Nicosia. Across the island, newly formed EOKA groups struck at military patrols and police stations.

Execution squads in the towns also gave evidence of increased efficiency as the organization turned its attentions to civilians suspected of giving information to the British. In one notorious case, a Greek Cypriot woman of middle age who had been publicly denounced as an informer was shot at her home in Famagusta. Although struck by three bullets, she survived and was removed to Nicosia General Hospital. A second gunman walked into the ward which she shared with thirty patients, and shot her, but he too failed to kill her.

The gunmen became increasingly bold in confronting members of the British forces, who now ventured into the towns only in groups and armed with automatic weapons. Within ten days, eight servicemen were killed or wounded by EOKA bullets while walking the streets in their off-duty hours.

One feature of Harding's design for the suppression of the rebellion signified to Grivas further evidence of the Machiavellian cunning of British politicians. On December 13, 1955, the Cyprus Communist party was proscribed and its leader and one hundred thirty-five arrested. In the small hours of the morning, several soldiers burst into the office of *Neos Democratis,* the party newspaper and seized the day's edition as it came off the presses.

The Communists still opposed the movement and its omnipotent backer, the Orthodox Church. Why then disarm an instrument with which the Cypriot people might be divided, if not ruled? British officials explained that there could be no freedom of action for an organization whose aims were "to prolong dissension and turbulence in the island"; but Grivas considered that the British needed the Communists to counterbalance EOKA. They were making martyrs of the entire party leadership. In fact, the Communists were not notably disturbed; many of their leaders who had been imprisoned were released in weeks or months; the party newspaper reappeared under another name; and Andreas Ziartides, the Communist leader of the island's largest trade union, who was abroad at the time of his party's proscription, took refuge in London;

this occasioned bitter comments from Grivas on the curious circumstance of a man "hunted" by the British in Cyprus finding sanctuary in Britain.

Grivas worked meantime to strengthen his guerrillas in the mountains. A group headed by Markos Drakos was based near the remote twelfth century monastery of Kykko, the largest and most powerful in Cyprus, which was to serve as a center of the courier and supply system. To the south, in the Pitsillia area, was another group headed by Renos Kyriakides. To assist him in establishing these guerrillas in the island's central mountain district, Grivas chose two other men: Andreas Chartas, a promising young villager; and Gregoris Afxentiou, the Greek Army reserve officer who had been in command of EOKA's Kyrenia district on the north coast. Afxentiou arrived within a few days to take up his new post with Grivas.

The British now began an operation to smoke out the mountain guerrillas, beginning with a search, on December 8, of every Orthodox monastery in Cyprus. They found only two revolvers and some sticks of dynamite. EOKA had been warned by its spies in the police and all supplies including the considerable stores held at Kykko, had been spirited away to safe houses and caches in the hills. From the pulpit, Archbishop Makarios denounced the "violators of holy places."

On the following day, the main British drive "Operation Foxhunter" began. Its target was Grivas himself. Grivas' headquarters above Spilia had been pinpointed by a renegade EOKA member who had met Grivas there.

On December 11 soon after dawn, a lookout woke Grivas with the news that British army trucks were entering the village of Spilia below them. A thick mist cut visibility to ten yards, and the lookout could see no more. By chance, Grivas' three top aides were all absent: Afxentiou on a reconnaissance patrol, Andreas Chartas visiting relatives at Polystipos, and Renos Kyriakides in Spilia itself, where he had gone to receive treatment for an injured hand and to make contact with a dentist who had been brought from the capital. Grivas was in agony with his teeth, besides which he was suffering from a heavy cold and sore throat. Only the previous day's steady downpour had prevented his going with Kyriakides to Spilia, where he would almost certainly have been caught.

Grivas posted additional lookouts, who reported movement of trucks and several hundred troops under cover of the mist. Afxentiou rejoined his chief to report that the army had captured Kyriakides and one of his men who was being forced at gunpoint to lead the way back to Grivas' headquarters.

Grivas sent three men, under Afxentiou, to an advance position with orders to open fire as soon as he saw the troops, and then to retreat to the main headquarters. Scouts reported that escape routes were not blocked, and Grivas planned to slip away to the west, where friends and fresh hideouts awaited them. It was three in the afternoon when Afxentiou saw the first commandos advancing in open formation up the mountainside, police dogs barking and straining among them. The captured man, roped to a soldier, was leading the way. Afxentiou opened fire, and the commandos answered his bursts with every weapon they had.

These troops were advancing from the south; but now a second British group was seen approaching from the north. As soon as Afxentiou rejoined him on the ridge, Grivas ordered a withdrawal westward, leaving the two patrols to fire upon each other in the mists. The guerrillas escaped without loss. The main road in the path of their westward march was unguarded, and they slipped across one by one.

Toward dusk, they rested briefly. But soon they heard the sound of a police dog. A patrol had tracked their footprints in the damp earth. It could not be more than ten minutes behind them. Grivas ordered the group to scatter. Each man must make his own way to Kakopetria village, the largest and most secure mountain village under cover of darkness. The men knew these hills and would have no difficulty in finding their way. The first ten men melted into the forest darkness while Grivas and three others brought up the rear.

Suddenly the guerrilla next to Grivas warned: "Look out, there's a soldier two yards away from you!" As the two men made off through the trees, two shots rang out behind them. The guerrillas did not fire back: the yelping of the dogs faded behind them; and they had no further contact with the army that night. Abandoning the paths, they struggled down rocky inclines, holding hands so as to avoid separation in the blackness. It began to rain. Again they crossed the unguarded main road, and saw no sign of the military. On December 12, at three in the morning they reached the heights above Kakopetria and waited for dawn to break. First light showed that the village below, and the horizons all around them were free from troops. They had escaped.

Grivas was astonished and encouraged by the British failure to cut off his retreat or to watch the main roads. The British, for their part, were well pleased with the capture of two guerrillas and the destruction of "a terrorist stronghold.'' Harding sent the commandos a message: ''Heartiest congratulations on your successes. All good fortune for the future.''

Two months later, on February 14, 1956, a forest guard accused of betraying ''the Castle'' to the British was shot to death by three masked men in the village coffee shop of Spilia.

— 9 —

Desperate Tactics

Grivas, who was now fifty-eight, was showing almost incredible stamina: he undertook long marches in the worst weather; he slept for a few hours in the open, and was ready once more for fresh dangers. By December 16, he had reestablished contact with the towns and issued new orders for action; and yet, his companions attest, he gave no sign of fatigue or depression.

But bad news awaited him at the new hideout near Kakopetria. An entire guerrilla group, that of Markos Drakos, had been shattered, its members killed, captured, and dispersed; and the debacle had been brought about by a lone British officer. Drakos had taken a group armed with Stens and machine guns to an ambush site on the coastal road. It was totally unsuitable, being without cover or good field of fire, and cut off from retreat on one side by the sea. Their first burst of fire wounded the driver of an army vehicle they had chosen to attack. But the officer beside the driver was unharmed; he returned their fire with a Sten automatic, wounding three men.

Drakos attempted to trick his opponent into the open by offering to surrender. He succeeded. But blood from a head wound was flowing into Drakos' eyes, and as the officer stepped out he fired his last rounds—and missed. Drakos scrambled for the top of a ridge, while bullets whined about him, and made off across open country.

The officer, Major Brian Coombe, covered the three wounded guerrillas—Haralambous Mouskos, who was dying, and Harilaos Michael, and Andreas Zakos until help arrived. Mouskos received a hero's funeral from the Cypriots, but Zakos and Michael were tried by the British, sentenced to death, and hanged.

70

Grivas kept up the EOKA attack with undiminished intensity. He gave district leaders across the island permission to choose and attack targets at will. The outcome was that an army officer was killed in an ambush; two soldiers were shot down in the street; police were killed; bombs thrown into a Nicosia restaurant wounded fifteen people, including two members of the American diplomatic corps.

On the heights south of Kakopetria on January 2, 1956, Grivas watched through binoculars as an informer led some eight hundred British troops in a thorough search of an area of a few square miles, an operation which was rewarded by the capture of an EOKA group, with their arms and ammunition. Although he scoffed to his companions at the unmethodical and wasteful fashion in which the British troops were used, he could not easily minimize the danger caused by these arrests, for on the previous day, Petros Stylianou, the leader of the captured group had visited his new headquarters and could reveal its location. The British were said to be extracting information by means of torture and the youthful Stylianou might at any moment divulge the secret. Grivas decided to move at once to Kykko. There Markos Drakos was again in charge. After his escape from Major Coombe he had been given refuge by an elderly village woman, who alerted EOKA. A doctor tended his wounds and now he had completely recovered.

Grivas, dressed in his usual thick grey jersey, marching boots and typical Cypriot villager's peaked cap, carried his M3 automatic, field glasses, and knapsack on the march over the northern slopes of Mt. Olympus. The journey took eight hours, and Grivas' two companions, Lambros Kafkallides and Harilaos Xenofontos, were exhausted before it was over. But Grivas urged them on through driving rain and over unsurfaced mountain tracks. At last they reached the great whitewashed pile of Kykko, where Drakos' hideouts were situated on the mountainside above the monastery.

The main hideout was a large trench dug into the mountainside and covered with branches and earth. Grivas greeted Drakos and his nine guerrillas. It was, for most of them, their first sight of the legendary "Dighenis." Exhausted as he was, Grivas made a speech urging courage and perseverance. They talked for a while, as the new arrivals ate bread and olives and drank water.

Next days Grivas divided the dozen guerrillas into two groups and gave instructions for new security measures. Approach routes to the hideouts must be constantly varied; boots must be covered with sacking

when entering or leaving a hideout to obscure footprints; no litter must
be left anywhere, not even a crumb that might attract birds; no open
fires must be lit, or lights used by night; hideouts must not be entered in
daylight except in cases of emergency; pepper should be spread around
the approaches to confuse tracker dogs.

Meanwhile, negotiations had been taking place between Harding and
Makarios, but Grivas was not optimistic about their progress: he could
not envisage that the British, in their present mood, would give even
a tentative promise of some future union with Greece. He considered
that Harding was setting a trap for the Cypriots, and he said as much to
the elderly abbot of Kykko, who visited him at the hideout one night.

Sir Anthony Eden, the British premier, was to meet President Eisenhower at the end of January 1956; and it seemed probable that the
President would be asked to put pressure on Greek Premier Constantine
Karamanlis, whose administration relied heavily on American aid, to
persuade the Cypriot leaders to make concessions to the British on the
grounds that the Cyprus conflict could damage the NATO alliance.

These considerations made it essential to keep up the attack; and yet
Grivas was unwilling to expose his guerrillas until their regrouping was
completed, both in the mountains and the towns. He turned to the
EOKA youth movement which provided the raw material for the fighting groups, and in an order of January 16, 1956, said:

> . . . young people must be ready to organize aggressive demonstrations
> if Harding decides, through arrests and searches of patriots, to attempt to
> pressure the Archbishop and the Greek Government into accepting the
> British Government's terms, or to influence the talks between Eden and
> Eisenhower. . . .[1]

The students performed their role with a will, constantly encouraged
by the harangues of Athens Radio. On January 7, the station broadcast
"a message from Dighenis [Grivas] himself," promising to continue the
struggle in bloodier form:

> . . . until the tyrant who desecrates churches, seizes the belongings of
> bread-winners and rapes virgins (yes, even that has been observed!) is
> driven from the land of our fathers. . . . On behalf of your fighting
> EOKA, children, I renew our sacred oath. . . .[2]

Harding appreciated no less than did Grivas that the bargaining advantage in the conference room lay with whoever was most successful

in the field, and while the skill of his forces had improved, he was not satisfied with the results. He wanted more men and better equipment. He lacked both a strong central reserve of troops from which to draw in emergency and any kind of clandestine organization through which EOKA might be infiltrated. He reported to the British government at the end of 1955 that the intensification of the conflict and the increase in casualties did not mean that the situation was deteriorating; on the contrary, the terrorists had been forced to show their hand and fight it out. There had been some encouraging successes, but much remained to be done. The Conservative government in London was in a mood to grant Harding whatever he demanded, and in January his security forces received a transfusion of several thousand men from England.

In the field, however, the British were becoming increasingly aware that numbers were of small avail against an organization that could dissolve into, and draw strength from, the people. What was needed now was better intelligence. The British introduced a body of men, both civilian and military, who had received over the years a long training in the arts of interrogation, culled from their experiences in a series of postwar troubles from Malaya to Kenya. The first of these men to come to the public attention were a captain in the intelligence corps, a veteran of numerous colonial rebellions, and his assistant, a twenty-five-year old lieutenant. In these early days of the conflict, when racial tempers were not yet fully inflamed by atrocity and propaganda, it was still possible to bring legal action against a British officer. Cypriot complaints, supported by the evidence of British policemen newly arrived from England, led to the institution of a court-martial against the two officers, who between them, had questioned hundreds of EOKA suspects.

A British inspector of police described finding Cypriots with bruises, swellings, and scars on their bodies after interrogation, and told how he had stood in a darkened hut listening to the sound of blows punctuated by repeated shouts: "Where are the caves?" "Who takes the food there?" A private soldier of the Gordon Highlanders described how he had been ordered to slap and punch a Cypriot suspect. He held him down while an officer beat the man over the back with an iron chain that was kept suspended from the ceiling.

Despite glowing tributes to the labors of these two officers from their commanders, and even from the governor's chief of staff, Brigadier Baker, who revealed that it was largely due to their efforts that the

EOKA gangs in the mountains had been broken, they were dismissed from the service.

In subsequent years, the question of torture was to become a major issue.

— 10 —

Makarios Is Exiled

Andreas Azinas had taken charge of arms smuggling in Athens following the discovery of the consignment of arms that had been concealed in a crate of religious books in December 1955. And now he needed time to build up a trustworthy new organization. Meanwhile, he improvised. First, he purchased an old metal bed and stuffed its hollow posts with ammunition and explosives, with the purpose of shipping it to Cyprus. To avert suspicion, he relied on the nature of his carrier, an elderly peasant woman: He gave her one pound for herself, and one pound to pay a porter; she kept both, and on her back carried the weighted bed aboard the steamer for Cyprus. It was safely received at Limassol by a Cyprus Transport Corporation driver and taken to the Archbishop's palace, where its contents were removed in a basement. At other times, Azinas hollowed out bars of thick green washing soap destined for a Nicosia orphanage and stuffed them with hundreds of rounds of ammunition.

On the island itself, EOKA sought out local sources of supply. A center of experiment was a small Nicosia chemist's shop which gave classes to student revolutionaries in the making of bombs. Here were devised a variety of simple weapons: the "Afxentiou cocktail," made from a mixture of potassium chlorate and sugar in a soft-drink bottle and detonated with sulphuric acid; or the "Springboard mine," constructed from sheet iron, planks, old car springs, and detonated by 6-volt flashlight batteries.[1]

Throughout the island turmoil and tension grew: from January 16 on, Grivas urged all groups to new efforts; and against the background of the wildest student demonstrations up to that time Harding flew to Lon-

75

don to meet Sir Anthony Eden. At the end of the month, the British
prime minister went to Washington to confer with President Eisenhower.

With all the major gymnasia closed down, and seventy-three elemen-
tary schools closed after the flag incidents, students marched through
the streets day after day, chanting for Enosis and EOKA. Soldiers fired
on one mob in Famagusta, killing the eighteen-year-old flag bearer, who
was also president of a local student body. The island went into mourning for his death, and four days later there came the inevitable reprisal.
On a Saturday afternoon, an execution group in Nicosia shot down three
British airmen in civilian clothes.

The capital was placed out of bounds to all off-duty servicemen and
turned into an armed camp. Patrols of troops in sneakers padded through
the streets at night with flashlights, or clambered over rooftops seeking
the elusive gunmen. Cypriots were herded into pens in school yards and
on playing fields, or kept lined up, hands on the wall, in the streets
waiting to be searched for arms. Barricades of wire blocked all entrances to the city.

But everywhere, by day, the bomb throwing and the rioting continued: a British housewife lost a foot in one explosion; an eighteen-year-
old Cypriot schoolgirl was shot in the leg during a "flag" riot. The
Voice of the Fatherland urged the youthful demonstrators on to fresh ex-
cesses:

> It is nothing if another year is wasted . . . even if many years are lost,
> even if the students remain illiterate, nothing is of value compared with
> the ideal which inspires them. When Cyprus is liberated, a statue of the
> Unknown Child must be erected alongside that of the Unknown Warrior.[2]

In the midst of this tumult, the Archbishop decided that he should
discuss with Grivas the latest British proposals and the future of
EOKA's campaign. On his return from London Harding had written to
Makarios offering, by way of a double negative, a tentative concession:
it was not now the position of Her Majesty's government, he explained,
that the principle of self-determination could never be applied to Cyprus; it was simply that it was not practical to apply it at present, in
view of the situation in the Eastern Mediterranean. The British offer was
of limited self-government; and Makarios must call for an end to violence the moment agreement was reached.

The Archbishop consulted widely among Cypriot community leaders and organizations, and was given almost unanimous support for his reply, which was to accept tentatively the offer to work out a constitution and further discuss points left vague by the British. Then, under the pretense of a few days "rest and meditation" in the mountains, he slipped up to Kykko for a secret meeting with Grivas. The arrangements were made by EOKA's leading courier, Loulla Kokkinou, a young secretary working for the Cyprus Transport Corporation, who with her sisters Maroulla and Ourania made up the leadership of EOKA's women's movement. Maroulla, the eldest, was married to a director of CTC, the island's biggest transport company, whose drivers regularly carried EOKA mail. The Kokkinou family had been involved in the Enosis movement from the start, but Loulla—a strong-willed young woman—had a streak of daring in her nature that marked her out for this kind of mission. She carried Makarios' outline of the new British proposals to Grivas and set with him the date and method of Makarios' arrival. The Archbishop, after a brief stay at the Trooditissa monastery drove at night over snowy roads to Kykko. Grivas appeared in the evening with his guards, and the two men talked in the abbot's study. Grivas considered the proposals vague and insincere. Above all, the British intention to keep control of internal security meant that they would not rest until EOKA had been wiped out. But the Archbishop won his agreement to a suspension of violence at least through the delicate final stages of the talks.

On February 15, Grivas called a halt to action, warning that this was only a temporary measure:

> . . . to facilitate the negotiations between the Archbishop and Governor Harding. Keep your guns loaded: be ready to hit back, if the enemy decides to strike.[3]

In the lull, differences between the two sides narrowed further. A Labour M.P., Francis Noel-Baker, came out from England, with Eden's approval, to employ his knowledge of Greek language and life in the role of mediator. The United States advised acceptance of the British offer. President Eisenhower had listened to Sir Anthony Eden, who ruled out the possibility of Enosis as a solution. The Turks made too great a contribution to the NATO alliance to be ignored; and neither Britain nor the United States "could afford to take Turkish friendship and understanding for granted." [4] Nor anyone else's friendship, for that matter: loyal Jordan had, that week, burst into riot and revolution, expelled General Glubb, British commander of the Arab Legion, and repelled Anglo-American efforts to make her join the Baghdad Pact. Another Western defense alliance was threatened, and the crumbling British position in the Middle East had to be shored up with America's backing. Archbishop Makarios need expect no encouragement from the United States in his search for better terms.

Three obstacles to settlement remained: the scope of an amnesty for EOKA members; the composition of the elected majority in any legislature; and the control of internal security. These, it was hoped, would be resolved by the personal intervention of Britain's colonial secretary, Alan Lennox-Boyd, who on February 26, 1956, flew out to join the talks. The Archbishop, Harding, and Lennox-Boyd were to meet on February 29, at the home of the Anglican archdeacon in Nicosia—a place chosen, perhaps, for its spiritual ambience—but before they could do so the peace of recent weeks was shattered by a series of explosions. Grivas, believing that a demonstration of EOKA's power at this moment would be a salutary warning for the negotiators, permitted one of his Nicosia groups to proceed with a scheme to "welcome" Lennox-Boyd with a salvo of grenades. Early in the evening, shortly before the crucial meeting, nineteen explosions echoed across the city, increasing the drama, but not heightening the prospects, of the conference. The archbishop described events at the Archdeaconry:

> The atmosphere was chilly. The Governor seemed hardly able to keep calm, and spoke only once, on the question of the police. Mr. Lennox-Boyd did most of the talking. First, we failed to agree on the amnesty, which I believed must include all political offenders: they did not wish to amnesty a large group. Mr. Lennox-Boyd had difficulty in explaining why the British must retain control of the police indefinitely. I said that a fixed period for the handing over of internal security should be laid down; it might be a month or a year, but a period of some sort should be made. Mr. Lennox-Boyd said, "The Governor will be able to explain why we must keep control of the police." Harding said, "You know why," and added that EOKA might continue to work underground and start up again later. I didn't see why, if we came to an agreement, EOKA should continue. I didn't like the way Harding put this issue: it was within his discretion to say when the police would be handed over. Then we briefly discussed the elected majority: they said a constitution would naturally provide for a Greek majority, but that details would have to be worked out by the legal experts who would draft the constitution. I said I was sorry that we had failed to reach agreement, and the meeting ended. I was not too worried, I expected we would meet again. But I noticed that for

the first time, Harding and Lennox-Boyd stayed on after I left. At all previous meetings, Harding and I had left together. I believe they decided on my exile that night, and sent the proposal to London.

As for the explosions, I was very angry. I did not want the British to think I was so foolish as to try to put pressure on them in this way. I believe the bombs hardened their view and contributed to my exile. I wrote an angry letter to Grivas next day, saying that he had spoilt everything, but the Abbot of Kykko, to whom I showed it, thought it was too strong so I changed the wording.[5]

Grivas, the Archbishop added, made some excuse about a failure of orders to reach the Nicosia group.

There was no single overriding reason for the failure of this conference. Mistrust on both sides; misinterpretation of the Archbishop's bargaining instincts; miscalculation of the British readiness for a showdown; the anxiety of Eden to preserve some semblance of imperial power—all these contributed to a collapse that was to prolong the struggle for four years. Makarios, Harding was sure, secretly controlled the EOKA movement; and it seemed obvious that if a military victory was to be won, removal of the head of the conspiracy was vital.

One week later, the Archbishop announced that he would leave the island for a visit to Athens and London to publicize the Cypriot cause. Shortly before his departure, he heard rumors that a meeting of top security officials had been called at Government House to plan the method of his exile.

Makarios could not believe it: what did the British hope to gain? But he asked his sister to pack some extra clothes. At the entrance to the airport, the Archbishop's Cadillac was stopped by the police, and he was driven to the far side of the airfield where two RAF Hastings transports waited. Makarios recalled:

An officer was waiting at the foot of the steps, and he very politely invited me aboard, like an air hostess. Apologetically, he explained that it was his duty to inform me, etc., etc., and would I like him to read the Deportation Order? I thanked him, and said, no, a copy would be sufficient. We waited for twenty minutes, and then Father Stravros appeared. "How nice of you to come and see me off," I said, "but how did you get in?" He said he had not come voluntarily. The officer asked him if he was the Bishop of Kyrenia; so we knew we would not be alone. The Bishop arrived with his secretary, Mr. Ioannides. I said that if Kyrenia was to be allowed his secretary, I should be permitted mine. Since Ioannides spoke no English, a Turk attempted to translate his Deportation Order, with strange results. It sounded something like, "The Governor is very pleased to have you deported. . . ." Ioannides said he was not pleased, some Special Branch officers came aboard and we set off. I thought it was unjust of the British to deport Kyrenia; after all, he had done nothing. . . .[6]

The bishop had in fact been about to sit down to luncheon when the police arrived at his palace. A rival to Makarios in ambition if not in intellect, he had never been admitted to the innermost councils of the revolution.

Their plane headed southeast, but no one aboard would tell the exiles their destination. After some hours, Makarios produced a pocket dictionary with a small map of the world. An officer silently placed a finger on Nairobi. They landed at a military airfield and were driven off in a limousine:

> They had papered over the windows, though whether this was to prevent us from seeing out or others from looking in, we could not imagine. It was very hot inside, and the Bishop of Kyrenia became distressed and tried repeatedly to open a window. He did not succeed. Finally we found ourselves in a wired enclosure—some sort of military camp. I could smell the sea. I asked a soldier if this were Nairobi and he replied, looking startled, that it was Mombasa.[7]

The Cypriot party boarded a destroyer, H.M.S. *Loch Fada,* and were given cabins in the officers' quarters, the Archbishop occupying that of the captain. The bishop of Kyrenia refused to sleep in his cabin, and spent a first night on the bridge. The others were seasick. Makarios ate a modest meal in the captain's lounge, and retired early. He had guessed where they were going:

> I said to one of the officers: "I think we are going to the Seychelles"; and he replied, "I think so, too."

The Seychelles are a scattering of remote islands in the Indian Ocean, appropriated by the British from France in 1815, and have served as a place of exile for political prisoners from British colonies around the globe.

At the governor's summer residence of *Sans Souci,* Makarios and his companions were to spend the next thirteen months. He regarded it as "a pleasant, if sometimes frustrating vacation, in a place ideally suited for meditation." [8]

— 11 —

Grivas Takes Command

Sir John Harding gave the official explanation for the deportations of March 1956: the Archbishop and his friends were "committed to the use of violence" and therefore constituted a major obstacle to peace. A selection of captured EOKA documents was released to the press, to prove the culpability of the exiles, and some bottles, said to be petrol bombs found in a kitchen of the archbishopric, were put on display. Many "interesting documents," officials murmured, had been found in a search of the Archbishop's rooms.

The United States had encouraged Eden to be firm, but from the viewpoint of Washington this was going too far. The U.S. ambassador in Athens passed to Greece the sympathetic concern of his government for recent developments in Cyprus, and praised the dignity and states-manship displayed by the Greek government. In Athens, following the deportations, one hundred and sixty-two people had been wounded in clashes with police; and America wished to show that while she had given her support to the British in negotiating a peace, it did not extend to approval for the kidnaping of the leader with whom they were nego-tiating.

Grivas was outraged by the inaction of the Greek government, but not displeased to take on the political as well as the military leadership. Makarios' abrupt removal would fan the flames of revolt and help to transform the whole island into a battlefield.

Among the multitude of attacks at this period, three especially enraged the British. The first was the destruction by a bomb of a Hermes airliner, shortly before it was due to take off with forty-four women and children aboard; the second was the assassination of a British police sergeant; and the third was yet another attempt on the life of the governor.

The assassination of Sergeant Gerald Rooney in Nicosia brought a seventy-two-hour punitive curfew to the Greek inhabitants of the capital. The authorities closed down thirty-five shops and homes in the area of the crime, immediately evicting their tenants. For three days and nights thousands of people were locked into their houses while troops marched the streets and perched on roofs and walls, guns at the ready. It was plainly the official intention to cow the populace into obedience. Large "collective fines" were levied on villages and towns that could ill afford to pay, but the sums exacted from house-owners, while doing nothing to discourage sympathy with EOKA, did much to foment hatred for the British.

Like Grivas, Harding was now free of restraints and riding the crest of a wave of confidence: he told a press conference on March 20, 1956, that the army had infiltrated EOKA and promised that the coming six months would see a big change in the security situation. But on the day he made this statement, EOKA penetrated Government House. It was accomplished in this fashion: Neophytos Sofocleus, a young man who was Harding's personal valet, had been conscripted in EOKA in January 1956 by old school friends. They planned to plant a bomb in Harding's bed. Sofocleus was to carry into Government House a flat, book-shaped bomb, concealed by a corset which would hold it flat against his stomach. The girl friend of an EOKA member supplied the corset, and Sofocleus strapped the bomb, already fitted with a time pencil, about his waist. He bicycled the few miles from Nicosia to Government House, and passed two army sentries, both of whom knew him by name, without a search. He hid the bomb in his bedroom.

While luncheon was in progress the following day, he again strapped the bomb round his waist, went to the governor's bedroom and slipped the bomb under the mattress. Back in his room he changed his clothes and left the building. Transport awaited him in Nicosia; he was to join the guerrillas near Kykko monastery.

But the governor's habit of sleeping with his bedroom window open saved him: the temperature fell sharply during the night, delaying the timing mechanism, which required a constant 67°F. if it was to detonate the bomb within twenty-four hours. It was discovered next morning when a servant turned back the mattress to air the bed and was later detonated in the grounds of Government House.

Sofocleus was declared a wanted man, with a price of twelve thousand dollars on his head; and the entire Greek Cypriot staff of Government House was dismissed.

Among the numerous "obstacles to peace" which the governor was now at liberty to suppress or destroy, Athens Radio "Voice of the Fatherland" program received his early attention. These exercises in revolutionary rodomontade put out by the station had advanced considerably since the first weeks of the uprising, when the station's apathy had so incensed Grivas. Now, day and night, broadcasts invited young Cypriots to "use the language the colonial powers understand . . . the language of blood, sabotage and dynamite"; and, while the British Parliament still discussed the ethics of the problem, Harding received from London the permission, and the necessary equipment, to jam the radio's transmissions to Cyprus. No longer need Harding hear himself described as "the new Gauleiter"; or "the Mau-Mau executioner"; his own propagandists now had the air to themselves to denounce the "cruel murders," the death, terrorism, and misery with which Cypriot homes were being poisoned by "Mr. Grivas." [1]

EOKA's propagandists, for their part, turned increasing attention on the island's British garrison, which for the first time had shown signs of the tension and frustration caused by the danger and monotony of service in Cyprus: caged in the dubious safety of comfortless camps, resented by the public at large, more and more British soldiers appeared to be employing needlessly forceful methods in pursuit of the elusive terrorists. The list of Cypriot complaints against the soldiers ranged from manhandling and brutality in the streets to theft and damage to property during curfew and search operations. From time to time there was more blatant evidence of military disaffection, such as the court-martial of four infantry privates who had thrown grenades into their officers' mess, wounding two officers.

On the slopes of Mt. Olympus, Grivas kept close control of the fighting throughout the island by his network of couriers. The number of acts of violence officially recorded during March was two hundred and forty-six, the highest since the start of the uprising. The mountain guerrillas, too, were not idle. Gregoris Afxentiou had led fifteen men in an ambush at a sharp S-bend in the road between Handria village and the army's mountain headquarters at Platres. Two commandos in their Land-Rover were wounded, as were three police officers of the Special Branch traveling in the second vehicle. Drakos' group mined a bridge near Lefka and raked an army convoy with machine-gun fire, killing one soldier and wounding others.

In the towns Grivas had less control over events. His decisions, written on fine paper that could be folded into the smallest possible space, had to be carried by hand to district leaders. He had no staff to assist with specialized problems; and while he could trust Church leaders like Bishop Anthimos of Kitium to carry on the propaganda campaign in the absence of Makarios, there was still no one with any military expertise on whom he might rely. The groups of assassins in the towns were especially wanton: they chose the easiest, and therefore least valuable targets; they attacked in such random fashion that gunmen wounded one another or were captured by unarmed bystanders. The first British civilian to be killed was shot on April 1, 1956—the anniversary of the start of the uprising. He had arrived on the island only two days before and was assassinated for no reason other than his nationality.

A more difficult target was Superintendent Kyriakos Aristotelus— "Kyriacoudi," the Greek Cypriot policeman who was loyal to the British and who resisted every threat and blandishment to make him change sides. EOKA tracked his movements, but bodyguards accompanied him everywhere and his office at police headquarters was in the heart of the Turkish sector, which EOKA entered at its peril.

Kyriacoudi was steadily breaking up the EOKA net inside the police force, which now consisted of some thirty men. It was Polycarpos Georgadjis, EOKA's intelligence chief, who eventually plotted his assassination.

On April 10, Kyriacoudi's wife gave birth to a son. EOKA agents who continued to watch the officer's movements reported that he went every evening to visit his wife and child at a Nicosia clinic; on April 15 he visited the clinic as usual. As he sat talking with a doctor in his office three masked men walked in, took Stens from beneath their coats, and opened fire. Kyriacoudi died instantly.

The outcry over this assassination obliged Grivas to issue a leaflet, declaring that the execution was performed on his personal order:

> . . . some circles have characterized the attack against Officer Kyriakos Aristotelus in a hospital as cowardly and immoral. This is foolish sentimentality. OUR SACRED AND RIGHTEOUS STRUGGLE COMES BEFORE ALL OTHER THOUGHTS. Those who are not with us are against us; and those who forget their national duty to the extent of acting against us will be punished! I have ordered the liquidation of traitors

whoever they may be and wherever they may be. The supposed sanctity of the places where they are will not save them.[2]

Within a month, the British executed Michael Caraolis and Andreas Demetriou, the first two EOKA men sentenced to death. At three in the morning of May 10, 1956, they were roped side by side to a steel girder in the execution shed of Nicosia Central Prison, and the trapdoor was released. The bodies were buried before dawn on the same day in a walled-off corner of the prison yard. Now, any hope that "moderate elements" among the Greek Cypriot community might come forward to negotiate with the British in Makarios' absence was finally dispelled.

Following the execution, Grivas announced that two British soldiers,—Gordon Hill and Ronald Shilton—captured by EOKA some time before, had been executed in reprisal. Hill had in fact deserted from his army camp in the Kyrenia hills four months previously. He was quickly picked up on a village road by EOKA guerrillas, who sent word to Grivas, asking what they should do with their catch. Before Grivas' reply arrived, Hill escaped from his guards, but he was soon recaptured. The EOKA men decided to kill him at once—he had seen their faces and their hideouts, and he was too dangerous to hold indefinitely. The guerrilla leader who had charge of this group at the time claims that Hill was shot; yet, at the inquest held when the body was discovered in a shallow grave in the hills ten months later, it was recorded that death was due to strangulation. In any event, the British had been unaware of his death in December 1955, and had posted him "absent without leave."

The second deserter, Ronald Shilton, fell into EOKA's hands in April 1956. He too was held for some weeks at a village house in Liopetri until, following the executions of Caraolis and Demetriou, Grivas sent orders to kill him in reprisal. As a guerrilla was later to confess in court, the "execution" was horribly bungled: the first shots only wounded the young soldier, a third smashed his jaw, and he was finally dispatched by a blow on the head with the shovel that had been used to dig his grave.

A leaflet signed by "Dighenis" [Grivas] was on the streets within twenty-four hours. It claimed the "execution by hanging" of Hill and Shilton, implying that both men had been killed together,

> . . . as a necessary reprisal for the judicial murder of Michael Caraolis and Andreas Demetriou, prisoners and victims of the British military dictatorship on this Greek island. . . . We shall answer hanging with hang-

ing and torture with torture. Hill and Shilton were buried in secrecy and
are not being returned to their own people, following the example of the
Occupation Forces towards the murdered Greek patriots.[3]

The riots in Greece, the depth of mourning in Cyprus were of a new
intensity; and in the political storm that followed, the government of
Constantine Karamanlis trembled before accusations of weakness over
Cyprus. Complaints by Grivas, the Cyprus Ethnarchy, and the Greek
opposition brought about the resignation of Foreign Minister Theotokis.
He was replaced by Evangelos Averoff, a man of independent mind and
Anglophilic sentiments which recent events had obliged him to revise,
at least symbolically: he returned to the British Embassy a medal (the
M.B.E.), awarded to him by Her Majesty's government for his wartime
services to the Allied cause.

— 12 —

The Hunt for Grivas

Grivas' agents in the police had warned him in May 1956 that Harding was preparing major operations centered on Kykko monastery, the guerrillas' supply base. That summer was to be the testing time for Harding's policies: the Archbishop's deportation had drawn criticism from the allies of Britain, and it had created a political vacuum which might best be filled by a British military victory. Intelligence had convinced Harding that the "hard core" of EOKA was in the mountains: the groups there offered a refuge for gunmen from the towns and provided the movement's romantic allure. Harding's chief of staff, Brigadier George Baker, settled on a four hundred square mile area of rugged mountain and forest as the area to attack. There had been incidents all round the edges of this region, yet none in its center: only at the village of Kambos near Kykko monastery, had there been an act of intimidation—the assassination of the village policeman. It seemed likely that Grivas was avoiding any confrontation there because it was the site of his own headquarters; and military intelligence knew that the road to Kykko was a main EOKA supply route.

Grivas was aware that the attack was coming; but from which sector he could not guess. He spread his groups over a wider area then he had previously occupied, personally leading two of them into the wildest area of the Paphos forest, known as the Mavron Kremas, or Black Chasms.

For ten days, Baker's force of paratroopers, commandos, and infantry redoubled patrolling in an attempt to drive the mountain gangs into a central area around Kykko and Kambos. On May 18 "Operation Pepperpot" began. Long convoys of troop trucks headed into the mountains, their lights out despite sheer drops into ravines at many points. The plan was to seal off a great sweep of mountainous terrain, with Kykko-Kambos at its heart. By dawn all roads out of the area were blocked by armored cars, and soon soldiers were everywhere, on hilltops, patrolling the donkey tracks, battling their way up ravines in the 100-degree heat of early summer. Villages were searched, Grivas' men held in wire enclosures, floors prodded with steel rods for hideouts, wardrobes and drawers turned inside out in every home. Great bins of flour and other foodstuffs were spilled on the ground. At this time, Kykko monastery was taken over as the army's headquarters.

With soldiers swarming everywhere, Grivas was often cut off from his sections and from Nicosia. Yet even at the height of operations, messages managed to arrive: Archimandrite Lefkosiatis, head of the Nicosia seminary, pleaded priestly duties at Kykko monastery to get through the cordon with news from the towns. He was not, however, allowed to leave; and Grivas' vital instructions for diversionary operations throughout the island awaited dispatch. Lefkosiatis instructed a young theological student to feign illness. He persuaded the army commander at Kykko that the boy must be moved at once to Nicosia. The British, anxious to show that people in curfewed areas were well treated, provided transport. The student carried Grivas' message concealed in the endpaper of a New Testament which had been slit open and resealed.

EOKA's diversionary attacks began next day, May 20, unleashing a flood of carnage that lasted until the middle of June. Nicosia began the onslaught by street bombings carried out by schoolgirls under Loulla Kokkinou's command.

The British responded with mass punishments. Fines totaling more than three hundred thousand dollars were imposed on a dozen small towns and villages. When Greek Cypriots complained that no such actions were taken against Turks who rioted and looted Greek property, the governor replied that the law was being administered "without fear or favour."

But diversionary attacks did little to distract the two thousand soldiers hunting Grivas throughout the mountains. "Pepperpot" continued for eleven days and nights, and Grivas was less inclined than he had been to scoff at his enemy's tactics: the enemy was making progress, and he must find new ways to meet the threat. Day after day he found himself estranged from Drakos and the other group leaders, without information or contact with Nicosia. They would have to move out before the advancing troops—if they had not been already encircled. But first they needed a guide who knew every hill and valley in this wild terrain. Grivas sent for Antonis Georghiades, the theological student from Athens, a group leader, and native of Milikouri, a village in the area. Grivas wrote in his diary:

> 27th May 1956: At about 0100 hours two couriers arrived with Benakis. When I got up I met him in the new area of our hideout (high up between the road Milikouri to Vassa and Kykko to Panayia). The question of our link to Nicosia and with the food suppliers was solved. . . . At about 1900 hours we left for the new hideout approximately one mile SW of height 4014. After a tiresome and extremely dangerous march we arrived at about 1115 hours next day. . . .[1]

Grivas came as near to death on this night march as he had ever been. The terrain was precipitous and covered with treacherous shale. Once Georghiades vanished over a cliff and tumbled twenty feet. His pack broke the fall. Then Grivas slipped and only saved himself from dropping into a ravine some hundreds of feet deep by grabbing a bush at the edge of the precipice. At two in the morning they rested for a few hours, then pushed on, pausing only to eat some bread and olives. Grivas was furious to find their radio receiver had been knocked out of order. They had lost contact with the outside world.

For a week they camped on a mountaintop in the area called Dipli, while the main thrust of "Pepperpot" spent itself in unprofitable searches. The radio was repaired, and they heard on CBS the official claim of seventeen "hard core" terrorists captured, along with "four complete village groups," fifty-two weapons, and much explosive. The guerrillas set about building a new hideout, sent scouts to reconnoiter possible paths of retreat, and reestablished contact with other groups.

Harding flew to London in June to sell his policies to the government and the people. He succeeded with little difficulty in both aims. Sir Anthony Eden was convinced that Harding's views were correct and the leader of the opposition acquiesced; the Treasury pledged funds and the War Office more men. The Foreign Office, the Colonial Office, and the military chiefs of staff were all briefed by Harding, in his capacity as field marshal, and in an address to three hundred members of both Houses of Parliament, he observed that there was little point in reopening negotiations with Makarios until the "terror gangs" were destroyed, which would occur before the year was out.

The British prime minister revealed to a Conservative party rally a new reason why Britain must stay in the island:

> No Cyprus, no certain facilities to protect our supplies of oil. No oil, unemployment and hunger in Britain. It is as simple as that today.[2]

On the face of it, there seemed little justification for Sir Anthony's alarmist attitude, except perhaps the need to give his Tory backers a popular slogan. But the thinking behind this new strategic view of Cyprus was soon to be revealed. On 26 July 1956 Egypt's Colonel Nasser nationalized the Suez Canal. Shortly afterward a buildup of Anglo-French forces began on Cyprus in preparation for the invasion of Egypt.

The British army meanwhile turned its attentions once more to Grivas with a new sweep—"Operation Lucky Alphonse." Thousands of troops swarmed over rocks and through forests sweltering in temperatures above 100 degrees. Every peak was manned by lookouts, watching for a hint of movement in the countryside; at night, scores of ambushes were set up. But once again the army had posted what Grivas called its "calling cards." At two in the morning he was awakened by the distant yelping of a dog. In that isolated place, with no village for miles, it could only be an army dog. It had wind of something. In the diary, he recorded:

> 8th June 1956: I woke my men and at about 0300 we left the hideout. When we reached the crest, and as soon as it was light, we observed four two-ton military vehicles full of soldiers going towards Milikouri. We saw them drop off on the way traitors Bouboulis and Botsaris (the code names of two captured guerrillas who were helping the British). . . .[3]

Grivas was seeking a height above a major road junction to the south, from which he could observe the area. Once the road was crossed, he and his four companions Antonis Georghiades, Pavlos Nikitas, Stylos Zapolitas, and Lambros Kafkallides could move south. They reached the hilltop in mid-morning and though Grivas scanned the horizon for an hour through binoculars he observed no sign of life. However, two scouts sent to reconnoiter heights to the east saw British sentries and trucks on the roads. The diary continued:

> After this I decided to shoot across the road Peravasa-Panayia, which we succeeded in doing. Although I noticed traces of fresh footmarks on the way and new empty English cigarette packets and realized that sol-

diers had passed that way, I decided to continue the march because there was no other way out. . . .[4]

In the evening they halted on high ground and turned in for the night. Two hours later they heard bursts of fire in the direction from which they had come; they assumed that a soldier was firing at a shadow or some animal in the darkness. At three the next morning they moved on, marching until dawn, then halted again, watching cars moving on the road below.

Grivas chose a crossing point on the road near an unguarded helicopter landing strip. The journey continued uneventfully until on Sunday, June 10, they reached Ayia Arka, an area well known to Georghiades. Now they felt sure that the worst danger was past. All morning they walked through the forest without seeing a sign of the army. They had nothing to drink but in the afternoon they heard the sound of running water and throwing caution aside for a moment they ran down the slope to the stream. When they were satisfied, Georghiades removed his boots, and Grivas sat down to write.

After an hour's nap, Kafkallides stood up to see facing him, across the chest-high scrub, a paratroop sergeant. As Kafkallides shouted a warning, a burst of fire came from farther up the stream bed. Grivas and the others ran for the trees, leaving everything behind. They worked their way to a hilltop a few hundred yards away and surveyed the scene. Patrols were hurrying down the mountainside in the direction of the firing.

Here Grivas exhibited his extraordinary ability to size up a dangerous situation. Instead of breaking out, as a less experienced commander might have done, he ordered his men to get into the undergrowth and wait until dark. It was only two hours off. No matter how closely troops came, no one was to move. He chose three thickly foliaged oaks and split the group up in a position that gave all-round vision.

They had left behind four pairs of binoculars, three automatic weapons, and Georghiades' boots. Grivas himself had lost his cardigan; his Sam Browne officer's belt, his reading glasses—in a case bearing the Athenian optician's name!—his beret, and his diary, at least the entries for the last three weeks. The British would surely know who was in their net. And yet the expected onslaught did not come. A patrol crashed about in the bushes, then left a guard some forty feet from where the guerrillas lay. A tracker dog with another patrol failed to pick up the scent. After an hour, the guard withdrew. Night was falling, but still they lay, covered with brambles and oak branches. The silence was broken at last only by the receding yelp of dogs.

The British who had occupied Kykko monastery alerted Government House of Grivas' whereabouts, and Harding poured more commandos and more infantry into the area.

Grivas called his men and moved off early in the evening. The danger ahead was the road that followed the river bed directly in their path. They were heading east now, toward the Pitsillia, where Afxentiou's group lay, and from which they had no reports of enemy searches. For hours they crawled uphill or eased themselves inch by inch down slopes: there must be no sound of falling stones or falling bodies. Shortly after midnight they reached the heights above the road, and found it un-watched. They waited for an hour in the darkness, but no movement was heard, no light flashed. They scuttled one by one across the open space, then moved down to the river bed. The stream was reduced to a thread at the height of summer and they crossed it quickly.

Shortly before dawn they reached a crest above the village of Kamin-aria. Grivas decided to stay there through the hours of daylight. Without food or water, they chewed grass to moisten their parched mouths. Georghiades—who had marched barefoot since the clash with the para-troopers—tore up the bottoms of his trousers to bind his bruised feet.

At sunset they moved down to the village and hid among rushes be-side a stream while Georghiades went to fetch food. The villagers were terrified: the army had been there all day, questioning every male. It had left only moments before the guerrillas came down the hillside. During that night and the following day, the group lay hidden in the tall reeds, slaking their thirst with bottles of water from the stream. At sundown of the second day, Georghiades and Nikitas headed for the village in search of food and walked into a commando ambush. Bullets whined all about them. They ran for their lives. Nikitas was hit in the foot, but after some hours they worked their way back to the others.

The group left at once, heading now for Trooditissa monastery, five miles to the east, eluding their pursuers. They saw behind them the beams of searchlights sweeping the area where they had evaded the pa-trol three days before. On June 13, they reached the monastery. The abbot provided food and clothes to replace their tattered guerrilla kha-kis. Grivas dispatched a monk to Limassol on foot—all transport had been banned from the roads—to explain that he was almost outside the army net.

They left the monastery at dusk, resuming the march southeast past army headquarters at Platres. Here a dozen resort hotels had been requisitioned to house officers, police, and senior officials handling the civil administration of "Operation Lucky Alphonse." The place buzzed with paratroopers and commandos, and the main north-south road through the mountains was busy with military traffic. But Grivas felt sure the worst was now behind them, and so it proved. They crossed the unguarded main road and toward dawn halted in a wood south of Troodos and slept out the day.

At night they pressed on, passing Mesapotamos monastery and halting at last two miles north of Saittas village. They would march no farther. In the morning, Grivas sent Georghiades to Limassol with orders to bring Demos HjiMiltis, the town's EOKA leader to Saittas; he was considering whether to join the groups under Afxentiou, or to go underground in the seaport of Limassol.

As he said goodbye to Georghiades, they saw behind them a rising pall of smoke covering the operational zone. The British army commanders, failing to find Grivas in the area where he had been spotted on June 10, had apparently decided on the expedient of starting a mortar fire to "smoke the guerrillas out." The risk of setting the forest afire was considered "justifiable" since it seemed impossible that the EOKA leader could have slipped through the net with thousands of men watching villages, streams, and paths.

On the morning of June 16, the mortar shooting began. Officers watched as shells burst in the remoter regions of the forest. Immediately, small fires broke out. A strong breeze fanned the flames, until fire was racing forward on several fronts. British forestry officials protested, but the army chiefs refused to allow the fire to be fought. Not until the blaze had been burning unattended for seventeen hours did the military concede that it was endangering lives, and allow in one hundred and fifty civilian fire fighters.

On the second day, several hundred troops were mustered to fight the flames, which now seemed likely to consume the entire four hundred square mile operational zone. At noon, when the wind was at its strongest, two columns of trucks packed with soldiers met head-on on a narrow mountain road. One column tried laboriously to back downhill, but the wind suddenly swept the fire up through a gulley at enormous speed. The trees on either side caught fire, and long tongues of flame poured across the road as if from a blowtorch. A few men, led by Cypriot fire fighters, ran to the open spaces of shale and lay face down. Nearly a hundred others were caught in the holocaust. When the worst was over and the flames had passed on, screams and the sound of exploding ammunition came from the smoke blanketing the road. Men began to stagger out, clothes and skin burned from their bodies. Because of the inaccessibility of the spot it was nearly twelve hours before some of the wounded reached a hospital. The final toll was twenty-one men dead and more than seventy injured.

At a court of inquiry later, some attempt was made to attribute blame for the fire to EOKA; but there was no evidence to support the charge, and in fact, no guerrilla groups were in the area at the time. Grivas was at Saittas, three days' march to the east. Markos Drakos, with seven men, had reached Yerakies village some twelve miles northeast of the fire by June 16. They had spent a week on the run north of Kykko before melting back into the population. Another group was captured on June 12.

Before "Operation Lucky Alphonse" ended, British commanders gave a press conference to announce its results. The soldiers who encountered Grivas on June 10 told their stories; the first captured photographs of the EOKA leader with his *andartes* [guerrillas] were released showing them posed in forest glades with their guns.

The British could claim that they had driven Grivas from the mountains, and had come within an ace of his capture. But it would soon be shown that the EOKA organization as a whole was not seriously affected. Throughout that summer, indeed, attacks on British forces increased in intensity, until in the "Black November" of 1956, EOKA reached new peaks of violence.

Was it merely a case of fortune smiling on Grivas and his men? The EOKA leader himself attributes his escape largely to the tactics of his opponents. Officers, he said, lacked initiative and judgment; other ranks lacked training, dash, and personal courage. The causes of their failure lay in gaps left in the net, the unwatched roads, which his party was able to cross five times in daylight unhindered. British movements were always visible, and guided the guerrillas' evasive actions. Tracker dogs gave warning with their barks, yet had trouble following a scent.

Grivas counted on the Cypriots' faith in the justice of their cause to keep the struggle going and restore the ranks of EOKA. "The British soldier, on the contrary, was well aware that he was fighting in order to keep a people in subjection . . . the upper hand would be gained by the one whose moral stamina was higher and his will stronger." [5]

— 13 —

Grivas Goes Underground

In answer to the summons by Grivas, Demos HjiMiltis, drove up to Saittas as soon as darkness fell, stopping outside an isolated cafe. The owner led him into the forest, where Grivas waited. He had decided against joining up with Afxentiou's guerrillas; instead he would go underground in Limassol, and HjiMiltis must find an appropriate hideout. HjiMiltis sped back to town and returned next day with his friend Nina, chief courier in the area, and Inspector Costas Efthymiou, a uniformed policeman, known as "Fat Costas" in tribute to his bulk; he would serve as their driver and escort. Shortly after midnight, with Fat Costas at the wheel, they moved off. All the guerrillas except Antonis Georghiades had been dispatched to their villages; Georghiades had proved more than useful to Grivas and he was to become his secretary, bodyguard, and companion for the remainder of the revolt.

The journey was uneventful. HjiMiltis in another car drove ahead scouting for trouble, but nothing disturbed the calm of the summer night. On the outskirts of Limassol, not far from the sea, they turned into a lane. The house, set well back from the road and screened by dense bushes, belonged to Dafnis Panayides, a market gardener who was one of the earliest members of EOKA. The fugitives were led into a small parlor with a framed text on the wall: "Home Sweet Home: where each lives for the other and all live for Christ. We dwell in Him and He in us. 1 John 4:13." Grivas thanked God "that we find ourselves among friends again." Panayides urged him to eat, but he would accept only a glass of fruit juice. He inquired about the construction of the hideout, its builders, and the number of the people who knew of its existence. At least fourteen, was the reply, but all were absolutely reliable. Grivas was dissatisfied. "God has protected us so far, but He cannot save fools," he remarked.

Panayides led him across a yard to a wooden shed that housed a large machine for cleaning and sorting seeds, which bore on a small brass plate the name of its British makers. In the middle of the shed reachable only by squeezing oneself through the machinery, was a concrete trapdoor. Panayides forced himself through and vanished down a dark, narrow hole.

Grivas followed down the ladder, into a room, twenty by ten feet, but with ample headroom. It contained two beds. Panayides demonstrated how a foot lever jacked up the trapdoor. A light bulb illumined walls and ceiling of pine planks, with two metal pipes for air vents which surfaced as the metal pipes supporting pergola over the drive. Work would start tomorrow on a lavatory and shower in the outhouse above.

Early next morning Panayides arrived with fruit and coffee to find his guests doing push-ups. While they ate, he explained that his family would keep watch on the road. There was an electric bell behind the boards of their hut. Three rings meant danger, one, the all-clear.

Grivas instructed Panayides and his wife Maroulla, whom he had already earmarked as a possible courier, to cultivate police friends and British acquaintances and to obtain what information they could without seeming overly curious. If EOKA called a strike, Panayides should go on working to show his lack of sympathy with the movement.

Soon the routine of the house was revolving around Grivas. Up daily at six, wash, dress, fifteen minutes of exercise, and not a minute less. Georghiades had to join in. Within two days messages began to flow in as contact was restored with district leaders. Never less than twenty a day arrived. A few important letters from Makarios or the Greek government were stored in jars and buried in the earth; the rest were given to Panayides to burn. Each letter was written by hand, and Georghiades might have to copy out a general instruction twenty times, for the various groups.

The house was screened by trees, and fields extended all around, permitting Grivas to walk in the yard in the evening. But there were too many children and visitors. He asked Panayides to find another place, and the gardener took a lease on a bungalow about two hundred yards away over the fields. Next a hideout must be built beneath it, and two suitable "housekeepers," preferably man and wife, found to live there and care for Grivas.

In his first messages from underground, Grivas called a halt to the diversionary attacks in the towns. At the same time he asked district leaders to prepare plans for further ambushes and sabotage which would not only show the British that they had failed to crush EOKA, but would raise Cypriot morale, and impress on Greek politicians his determination to accept no compromise.

Harding had returned from London on June 22 and instigated new searches. Operations dragged on through July, but the army's haul was negligible: a few villagers arrested, some guns and explosive seized. The press reported rumors that Grivas was dead or wounded, or had left the island. It was observed that EOKA leaflets had been distributed in Limassol without the customary signature of "Dighenis." This was a device used by Grivas when he considered that the British were getting too close for comfort. When the famous code name failed to appear, rumors began to spread. "The gentlemen of the press," Grivas noted, "are easily deluded." [1]

The government in London still hoped that Grivas would be caught. Sir Anthony Eden said that a new constitution for Cyprus would be introduced, but only after terrorism had been put down. Lord Radcliffe, a noted jurist, would visit Cyprus to draw up this constitution, although it was plain that no one from the Greek Cypriot community would accept it so long as Archbishop Makarios remained in exile.

Attacks by the guerrillas continued at a fast pace throughout July and into August. The incidents that caused most stir in Britain were the urban guerrillas' daylight killings in the towns, which neither curfews nor increased patrols were able to stop. In the length of Nicosia's Ledra Street, nicknamed "Murder Mile" by British newspaper correspondents, there were sometimes as many soldiers as civilians, but they knew neither from where the next attack would come, nor how to meet it when it did. Justice Bernard Shaw, who had condemned to death the EOKA martyrs Caraolis and Demetriou, was ambushed only a few hundred yards from the Nicosia courthouse. The bullets of two gunmen shattered his car window, piercing the judge's throat; the judge's armed escort leaped out and exchanged shots with the gunmen, but they escaped. Shaw's life was saved by a prompt operation.

EOKA's campaign against suspected informers was intensified. Six were assassinated in June, twelve in July (including three women), ten up to the middle of August. The commonest place of "execution" was also the most public—the village coffee shop—to warn those who might be tempted by British rewards for information. For this form of warfare, no textbooks existed; its adolescent practitioners had to devise their own tactics through trial and error.

A Nicosia EOKA group headed by Nicos Sampson, a young journalist, was given the task of rescuing Michael Koutsoftas, a guerrilla, who had been condemned by the British to the gallows. When it was learned that Koutsoftas would visit Nicosia General Hospital for an x-ray, Sampson, with four men and two girls, entered the hospital, kidnaped a manacled prisoner from guards at gunpoint and escaped in their small car. It was only when they reached an outlying village where the condemned man was to hide that they discovered that the wrong man had been rescued: their prize was Argyros Karedemas, a Greek national who had been captured aboard the arms smuggling caique *St. George* in 1955. Karedemas was sent to join the re-formed guerrilla groups in the mountains.

EOKA did not care to admit an "error." But when a U.S. vice consul, William P. Boteler, a young diplomat from Washington, D.C., was killed by a bomb thrown into a restaurant, and three officials of the U.S. foreign service dining with him were injured, Grivas issued a leaflet expressing Cypriot regret at this "tragic error." Press reports had represented this event as a premeditated attack on Americans. "No Greek," said the leaflet, "could bear hatred for the American people, whose liberal sentiments, taken as a whole, must put them on our side in our righteous struggle." [2]

Whatever the sentiments of the American people, the administration in Washington continued to favor the Anglo-Turkish view of the question: these allies were more stable and more dependable than was Greece, and they contributed far more to Western defense. For some time the philhellenic statements of Cavendish Cannon, Foster Dulles' ambassador in Athens, had irritated British leaders, and in July 1956, he was replaced by George Allen, a former undersecretary of state, who openly took the view that no proposed settlement in Cyprus should be allowed to endanger American friendship with Turkey.

The government in Athens was under pressure to abandon its campaign at the United Nations. The advent of Allen signified a new American determination to hold Greece—a land heavily dependent on U.S. aid—to its NATO commitments and stand by Britain and Turkey in their refusal to consider the island's demand for self-determination. The Cyprus problem was a cross not willingly borne by the administration of

Constantine Karamanlis, which was under attack for its failure to take a bold stand against the common front of Britain and Turkey. Karamanlis now began pressing Grivas—through his consulate-general on Cyprus—to declare a temporary truce in which parleys might start. A one-sided cease-fire would answer the British argument that "EOKA violence" was the sole obstacle to a settlement. That same month, Sir John Harding, in an interview with the *Times of Cyprus*,[3] had said: "If there is to be a stopping of violence and its consequences in this island, I can only say: Let the murderers make the first move."

Although barely a week had passed since the hangings of the young EOKA members at the Nicosia Central Prison and the island had just emerged from a general strike called in protest to their execution, Grivas decided to bow to the wishes of Athens. By "creating an atmosphere of peace," he would "leave the field open for diplomacy to find a political solution to our troubles."[4]

On August 17, 1956, leaflets announced that EOKA was suspending, unilaterally, all operations so that Cypriot demands, as set out by Archbishop Makarios, could be discussed. The organization, meanwhile, would "stand guard, ready for new sacrifices, knowing that it has all the moral and material backing necessary."[5]

The proclamation caused worldwide interest. Hopes for peace were raised for the first time since the deportation of Makarios and crowds of celebrating Cypriots flowed into the streets to mingle with British troops. The bishop of Kitium, the Archbishop's deputy, declared his hope that Makarios could now be released to commence fresh negotiations; and Sir John Harding, before consulting London, said the EOKA move could be a turning point in the island's history and an opportunity to make a fresh start.

— 14 —

No Surrender

In London, the Conservative press depicted the cease-fire as a ruse to save EOKA from dissolution before its debility was exposed; it would then use its remaining strength to terrorize moderates when political talks resumed.[1] The Conservative government of Sir Anthony Eden plainly regarded the offer in the same light, for after a silence lasting seven days the British replied with a demand for the surrender of Grivas and all his men.

The "surrender terms" gave the terrorists three weeks to give themselves up with their arms: they could then individually choose either to be exiled for life to Greece, or stay in Cyprus and be detained for whatever term the governor thought fit. Those suspected of specific acts of violence against the person could also expect to face trial and, presumably, execution under current laws.

Even without Grivas' immediate rejection of this demand, it may be doubted whether any guerrilla would have been tempted by such unattractive terms. To the EOKA leader they reflected Harding's determination to win an absolute military victory in the field and impose his government's will on the Cypriots.

The surrender terms had been announced on the evening of August 22, 1956: on the following morning Grivas' reply was made—in the shape of leaflets thrown from speeding cars, from rooftops, and by school children on bicycles.

The document, defiantly headed VICTORS DO NOT SURRENDER, recalled the words of the Greeks of Thermopylae when invited to throw down their arms, and held out a similar invitation to the British to "Come and get them, if you dare."

101

The British demand shows insincerity and malice: but in order to manifest my goodwill once more, and to try to avert further bloodshed, I notify you that if this treacherous demand for surrender is not withdrawn by midnight on the 27th instant; and if negotiations do not begin on the terms laid down by Archbishop Makarios, then I shall cease to be bound by the ceasefire, which I declared on my own initiative, and I will resume liberty of action.[2]

Grivas simultaneously sent out orders to all district leaders to prepare for immediate action. The world was watching for their reaction, he warned, and their slogan must remain: "Freedom or death!"

A curious propaganda battle now ensued. Light aircraft of the RAF circled the towns, giving instructions through an amplifier to surrender and showering leaflets on the heads of a startled public. EOKA gave a derisory reply. A donkey was turned loose to wander in Nicosia with a placard around its neck reading I SURRENDER. Banners were draped over the walls of the local sports stadium: "ALL FIGHTERS ARE AT THEIR POSTS." The same message was shouted through megaphones by EOKA men to village crowds. No one surrendered.

Two hours after the end of the cease-fire, at midnight, a bomb was thrown at the house of a British serviceman; and next day a gunman shot down an army officer in the street. The conflict was on again.

Grivas, however, had ordered only a limited campaign of activity for the present: nine fresh British infantry battalions had arrived in Cyprus since Nasser's nationalization of the Suez Canal on July 26, but they were not being used against EOKA. It seemed probable that Eden was planning some kind of action against Egypt; Grivas would reserve EOKA's strength until the British forces were diverted to Suez, and then strike. But now the government in London engineered a propaganda coup which demonstrated for the first time the depth of Archbishop Makarios' personal involvement with EOKA. By publishing extracts from Grivas' captured diaries, the Conservative administration hoped to silence criticism of its policies by the Labour opposition and embarrass the Greek government with proof of its complicity in the revolt.

Grivas was a compulsive diarist: even when hotly pursued in the mountains he had not failed to make daily entries in a series of notebooks. The captured portions gave a detailed account of the creation of EOKA from the autumn of 1954 until the summer of 1955, with a few further entries for the summer of 1956.

On the day the British released details of these papers, Grivas made a fresh entry:

> 27 August '56: The first impression is deplorable. The morale of the people has suffered a shock. To raise it . . . I have put out leaflets saying that the whole story of my journal has been fabricated by the British in order to distract world attention from the situation in Cyprus which they themselves have created.[3]

The diaries, along with many letters, orders, and memoranda, had been deposited in glass jars and buried in two separate caches in Nicosia and the village of Lysi. Grivas suspected that they had been turned over to the British by one of his former housekeepers and by a Nicosia watchmaker whose shop had been used as a clearing house for EOKA messages. When investigation appeared to confirm this, he had the watchmaker, Andreas Lazarou, killed by the execution teams. But the housekeeper, with his wife, sought British protection and was shipped out of the island with whatever reward the Cyprus government saw fit to give him. Up to ten thousand pounds had been offered for this kind of information.

What the diaries meant to the British government was revealed by the colonial secretary, Alan Lennox-Boyd, who cast the Archbishop as the villain of the piece—determined to impose his solution by force on the unwilling islanders. There could be no question of his return in any capacity until terrorism had been eradicated.

Her Majesty's Stationery Office issued a handsome illustrated booklet of ninety pages giving extracts from the captured documents, and appended some details of "terrorist atrocities," in order to demonstrate "to what ugly and bestial reality fine words and exhortations have been translated."

The British surrender terms remained open until September 12, and Grivas kept up a leaflet campaign throughout the period, mocking "the satrap"—the "Field Marshal of the Mau-Mau"—who sat in his palace on the hill awaiting the surrender of EOKA fighters; he had promised to crush the organization in six months, said Grivas, but EOKA was now making more powerful attacks than ever; and far from surrendering, his men were escaping from prison to fight again.

Polycarpos Georgadjis, the ex-leader of Nicosia, had escaped from prison after a bloody gun battle on the grounds of the general hospital.

Faking stomach illness in his prison cell, he had been sent to the hospital for an x-ray. Andreas Chartas, the town commander, on learning this from a message smuggled out by a wardress, summoned Nicos Sampson, a group leader, to lead a commando-style raid and snatch the captive from his guards. Sampson, with three other EOKA men and two girls, drove at once to the hospital. They found Georgadjis between two British sergeants and two Turkish warders in the entrance hall. Sampson pulled a revolver from his belt, and a wild exchange of firing began. One of the sergeants, hit in the stomach, sprayed the crowded hall with machine-gun bullets as he fell. The other traded shots with Sampson as Georgadjis slipped from the handcuffs that secured him to a warder and ran.

In a matter of minutes, fifty bullets had been fired, and four men— two of Sampson's fellow gunmen, a police sergeant, and a Greek-Cypriot bystander—were killed. Several others were wounded. Georgadjis who was nearsighted could not see the EOKA girls waiting in a car outside the hospital and ran through the streets. Eventually he found refuge in the home of a Greek timber merchant, whose wife alerted EOKA. The Kokkinou sisters arranged for the hunted man to be removed by a policeman who was also an EOKA member.

Sampson and his group made off in their car. Stopped at an army roadblock, Sampson ordered the girls to hide their guns beneath their skirts; and when their turn came to be searched, he seized the girl beside him and began to kiss her. The officer in charge peered through the window, murmured something about "young love" and let them pass.

EOKA's gunmen in the towns now moved to the forefront of the activity. Informers were being eliminated indiscriminately in the wake of the capture and betrayal of Grivas' diary, and Grivas had ordered renewed street attacks on British servicemen. There were thirteen killings in the first two weeks of September, and when, on September 20, three more EOKA men were executed in the central prison, reprisals were inevitable.

Nicos Sampson showed his ability as an "executioner" who always pressed home an attack. The guerrilla assassin, as Grivas appreciated, required "courage, initiative, rapidity of thought, and physical strength." [4] Long hours must be spent observing a victim's habits, his precautions, and the guards along routes he used. The police, for their part, had issued a list of precautionary measures to be taken by British civilians, ranging from "avoiding routes which might lead into traffic jams'' to always carrying a weapon in a shoulder holster rather than a pocket. No Briton was unaware of the danger he faced in walking the streets.

Grivas ordered that an executioner should never carry his own weapon; some person not liable to suspicion, such as a schoolboy or a woman, must act as carrier and dispose of the gun to a third person able to escape from the killing zone—usually cordoned off in a matter of minutes by British forces.

Sampson's personality made him a natural leader of the Nicosia groups. Born in Famagusta of well-to-do middle-class parents he had been active in street rioting before joining the Greek Cypriot newspaper *Phileleftheros* (The Freedom-Lover). He had been picked out at one demonstration as a ring leader and sent to jail for several months. At twenty-one, he was the driving force that summer and fall behind the street killings which outraged British sensibilities. He had already taken part in the executions of several informers and one British army corporal who was shot down in front of his wife in a Nicosia grocer's store.

Now, after the triple hanging on September 20, Sampson and his group were told to carry out a reprisal. Using his favorite weapons (a Webley and Scott .38 revolver of the type issued to the police), Sampson worked in spurts: two or three executions on successive days, then perhaps a week to recuperate, then another burst. Time, to him, was of the essence: he could allow a limit before he vanished of up to two minutes to make sure of his victim after the first shot was fired. The shock effect, even on armed British bystanders was such that few assassins were shot in flight.

The gunmen usually worked in pairs. It was not always easy to deliver a fatal wound, and survivors could often identify their attackers (one man lived with thirteen bullets in him). It was decided that maximum efficiency could be reached by "softening up" the victim with a bullet in the stomach or lower back; he could then be finished with a shot through the side of the head above the ear. But such theoretical approaches to the problem often went astray in the bloody moment of decision.

In the week following the hangings the Sampson team killed first a British army captain, whose movements they had studied for some time: the gunmen waited with two girl gun carriers at a small cafe adjoining a road junction where the officer's car was obliged to halt. He passed that way at about the same hour each day. It required little courage and less skill to shoot the man in the head, through the open car window, as his car stopped at the white line. Only later did Sampson discover that the victim was an army doctor, and therefore—like so many "opportunity targets"—not a particularly apposite choice for assassination. These random slayings were later to take the lives of many harmless civilians, including British journalists sympathetic to the Greek-Cypriot cause. Sampson's superiors plainly considered the outcry in Britain useful to their cause, for the young gunmen continued to be given a free hand.

Grivas wrote a justificatory disquisition on the street killers in his *Guerrilla Warfare:*

> Our opponents called us murderers because we struck from behind. Such a charge is, to say the least, naive, because to kill your opponent by assailing him at his weakest point, from the side or the rear, is a tactic as old as . . . Marathon. What would the critics say if a general were to make a frontal attack against a much stronger opponent, thereby leading his soldiers to a useless death? They would of course demand that he be court-martialled or at least cashiered.[5]

The gunmen, in Grivas' view, were simply employing correct military tactics on a smaller scale.

It may be worth considering in detail the "centerpiece" of Sampson's career as an assassin, the shooting of three armed policemen in Nicosia's main street, since this required some enterprise. The choice of victims was not entirely fortuitous: armed, but wearing plain clothes, they had entered a shop that morning to buy cameras and exchanged words with the manager. "We came to Cyprus to catch Grivas," said one. "We'll crush EOKA like that." He crumpled a cardboard container in his fist. Working at the shop was one of the lookouts for Sampson's team: he roused the gunmen and explained what had been said.

Sampson and two others, Athos Petrides and Andis Tseriotis, found the policemen window-shopping in Ledra Street. He told his companions they would come up on them from behind and each pick off one man. The three police officers—William Webb, J. W. Thoroughgood, and J. P. Carter—were walking in single file along the narrow street busy with pedestrians and traffic.

Sampson shouted to his two men to fire. Together he and Petrides shot Carter and Thoroughgood, but Tseriotis, who had never before fired a gun, was slow to react, and when he did get off several bullets, they struck Webb in the arm. The crowd scattered, screaming. Sampson and Petrides ran. Round the first corner, they heard more shots. Sampson turned back and found Tseriotis standing in the street with two dead or dying men some yards away.

Thoroughgood raised himself on one arm and fired three times. One bullet hit a fleeing Cypriot in the leg, another buried itself in a doll hanging by a toyshop door. Then Webb stood up to fire as Sampson dragged Tseriotis round the corner. Sampson slapped the youth across the face to bring him to his senses and half-carried him toward their waiting car. Carter and Thoroughgood died a few moments later; Webb sat on a doorstep clasping his gun, with blood running down his arm.

It was more than an hour before curfew descended on the city. By that time the killers were thirty miles outside Nicosia, heading for the monastery of St. Andreas, at the easternmost tip of the island. Sampson had been seen by dozens of people, many of whom knew him by sight.

The curfew was maintained for a week. The population was locked indoors—but for a brief interval to buy food—day and night. Troops threatened to shoot anyone who put a head out of a window. Newspapers could not appear, and Cypriots lost family income calculated at well over a million dollars. This was the severest collective punishment of the conflict: hundreds of Cypriots were marched from their homes to barbed-wire pens where they were interrogated. Some spent two or three days waiting their turn. Food ran short and long lines waited in the daily break to draw water from public fountains.

The administration insisted that the curfew's purpose was "to assist the security forces in their investigations," but no guerrillas were arrested. Over the next four months, Nicos Sampson would preside at a dozen further "executions."

— 15 —

Black November

The new underground hideout which the Limassol guerrillas had been preparing for Grivas was ready by mid-September, 1956. The small stone cottage sat in open fields within sight of the Panayides' land, screened from the road by a line of pomegranate trees. Market gardens and vacant lots lay all around. In the backyard a patio—rather larger than was usual in Cyprus—contained trashcans and a British motorcycle. Beneath it lay the new hideout.

The housekeeper found for Grivas was Marios Christodoulides, a young man who worked for branches of the Ottoman Bank inside the bases of Akrotiri and Episkopi, seat of British Middle East Headquarters. Deferential, quiet, and fluent in English, Marios was considered by his British superiors to be "the right kind of Cypriot."

Neither he nor his wife, Elli, hesitated when youth leader Manolis Savvides asked them if they would hide some wanted men. When it was explained that the guests would include Grivas, they were at first appalled; but Savvides persuaded them, saying that it would be only for a few months.

Work on the hideout progressed by night under the guise of building a septic tank. It was lined with planks and a shaft sunk from the kitchen to a depth of twelve feet; from this point a tunnel six feet long led to the underground room. With access to the hideout from the house, work proceeded more easily than at first; weatherproofing was brought in, the tunnel was plastered and whitewashed, a permanent ladder fixed in the shaft, and a jack was installed to raise and lower the heavy concrete trapdoor. Above this door was a kitchen sink with a cupboard. A long pole, jammed up against the trapdoor from beneath, dulled the hollow sound if searchers tapped the floor.

Electricity was taken down through the wall behind the kitchen meter and the cellar lit by a 200 watt bulb in the ceiling. A small fan kept the air moving and air vents at the surface were disguised in a border of hollow ornamental bricks. On the concrete roof of the hideout, Marios parked his car. Chickens, pecking about its wheels, provided a final touch of rustic authenticity.

Grivas did not live entirely underground. A pleasant, upstairs work-room had been prepared for him and his aide, Georghiades, with a table and chairs, couch, and bed. The shutters were always closed, and Grivas would often peer through to where less than one hundred yards away, beyond the pomegranate trees, a Union Jack fluttered above an army school. It was under guard throughout the day, and Grivas had to become accustomed to soldiers wandering down the lane to pick fruit. Christodoulides' dog Irma, tied to an apricot tree by the front door, gave warning of their approach.

The doors of the sink cupboard were kept closed, and packets of cleanser placed on the trapdoor. Grivas timed a trial run of an emergency descent: five seconds to sweep aside the packages, grasp the edge of the sink and swing down feet-first into the shaft; twenty seconds to jack the door back into place on its hinges. In less than thirty seconds he had vanished underground. The cellar was fitted out with two narrow camp beds, shelves, a trestle table for writing, and a small desk radio. One could, if need be, remain there for weeks at a time. Nothing of an incriminating nature was kept upstairs. Clothes, papers, guns, and large-scale maps of the island stayed in the hideout.

From the day of Grivas' arrival, the routine hardly altered. At six in the morning, he and his aide emerged from the hideout, washed, exercised, breakfasted; and Marios brought the newspapers before going to the bank. Then Grivas and Georgiades worked in the front room of the house, drafting leaflets, writing letters and orders. Supper was at seven; afterward Grivas took his evening stroll in the dusk outside the house, up and down, up and down, on the side away from the road. Occasionally Georghiades paced with him. In times of crisis, all three—Grivas, Georghiades, and Marios—would be up until two or three in the morning, writing and typing.

Elli Christodoulides soon found that her guests—like her nine-month-old daughter Miria—could not be left to look after themselves. A chance caller might appear and every moment of the day she had to be watchful.

Visitors were few, apart from the daily arrival of EOKA's mailman—HjiMiltis, his wife, one of the Panayideses, or Andreas Papadopolous, one of the builders of the hideout. No others knew Grivas' whereabouts. As many as sixty messages a day might go out from this headquarters, typed on the thinnest paper and bound together with transparent tape to make the package as small as possible.

Grivas encouraged Marios to cooperate with British employers and clients at the bank. He held the keys to the safes, controlled curfew passes for thirty-two bank employees, and scrutinized the accounts of senior officers such as General Boursne, C-in-C Middle East Land Forces, and Air Vice Marshal Weir, the RAF's Mid-East commander, with whom he sometimes spoke.

For more than two years, Grivas would lead the struggle from these surroundings. Now, in September 1956, events were approaching a climax: the large number of British and French troops flowing into Cyprus indicated that an attack on Suez was imminent, while renewed diplomatic activity over Cyprus was under way in London, Athens, and at the United Nations. Soon the proposals of Lord Radcliffe for limited self-government would be made public and pressure was being put on Grivas by the Greek government to declare a new cease-fire. But EOKA was, in fact, about to begin its strongest attack of the conflict.

The Anglo-French adventure in Egypt was launched on October 31, 1956, and British troops were dispatched from Cyprus for landings at Port Said. Thus, pressure on EOKA relaxed as some six thousand troops were withdrawn from operations in the Kyrenia and Troodos mountains.

This was the moment Grivas had long awaited, and the reason he had fended off all suggestions for a new cease-fire. The Greek government considered that a new truce would be politically advantageous if declared immediately after the inscription of Cyprus on the United Nations agenda; while Noel-Baker, the Labour M.P., in a personal letter to Grivas, also appealed for another truce. He had reason, he said, to think that such a "bold and realistic gesture" could not, this time, fail to bring about a lasting peace.[1]

Grivas thought otherwise. Sir John Harding, he was sure, was dedicated to the idea of a military victory; and the British government would seize on the truce as a means of avoiding a confrontation at the United Nations, arguing that international debate was no longer needed now that the way to direct negotiations lay open. Grivas rejected the truce suggestions and launched his new onslaught. Guerrillas ambushed army trucks, blew up military and harbor installations, raided police stations, and killed soldiers and civilians alike. Cypriot sympathies were with the beleaguered Egyptians, and Grivas did what he could to upset the Anglo-French air attacks on the canal zone by ordering sabotage at the RAF's Akrotiri base from which the raids were launched. A Cypriot workman smuggled four time bombs hidden in a basket of grapes into the camp, then crawled down a stormdrain with the bombs slung around his neck. The job, which involved long waits while British sentries patrolled the area, took six hours to complete, but ended in success. The explosion blew large gashes in a main runway, putting it out of action for several days.

Bombs fixed in the branches of trees close to roadsides were electrically detonated from a distance, causing severe head wounds. A parcel bomb, disguised as a book which exploded on being opened, killed the British district commissioner of Platres, as he sat at his office desk.

In a mountain area which only days before had been swarming with troops, Markos Drakos' guerrilla group ambushed three army lorries, sending two vehicles off the road. Soldiers returned the fire and attempted to shell the EOKA positions with mortars. In an engagement lasting some fifteen minutes, a British sergeant was killed and three soldiers wounded. The guerrillas retreated without loss.

The urban guerrillas were the most active of all. By this time, Nicos Sampson had played a role in more than a dozen killings: he had led the ambush of an army truck at a busy road intersection in Nicosia, killing a British warrant officer, and almost losing his own life under fire from a truckload of paratroopers which arrived by chance.

He also killed a noted British journalist, Angus MacDonald, who had come to the island only a few days previously from the London *Spectator* and had joined the *Times of Cyprus* staff. Sampson saw the young Englishman walking the streets and assumed him to be a "special constable," like two British businessmen who had been murdered earlier that month. But whereas the latter were armed and were outspoken opponents of EOKA, MacDonald carried no weapons and had written articles highly critical of official British attitudes. The assassination embarrassed Cypriot leaders; there were complaints inside the EOKA hierarchy and Sampson's star began to fade. The young journalist was his last British victim.

While the Anglo-French venture in Egypt lasted, EOKA missed no opportunity for attack. During "Black November," as it was called by

the British, there were four hundred sixteen incidents, the highest
monthly figure to date, and of the forty people who lost their lives,
twenty-one were Britons. Sir John Harding's response was to extend the
range of offenses for which death must be imposed. Judges were now
required to pass a mandatory death penalty on everyone convicted of
discharging firearms, carrying arms, throwing bombs, possessing or
manufacturing explosives, or consorting with anyone who did so. The
governor also assumed the power to suppress any newspaper; at the
same time the people lost their right to prosecute members of the police
and armed forces if they had been ill-treated. A complainant might seek
from the attorney general a special dispensation to prosecute, but if his
complaint was later rejected—after an inquiry conducted by colleagues
of the man or men accused—he might then be imprisoned for three
years, or fined one hundred pounds.[2]

— 16 —

Harding Strikes Back

With the end of the Suez operation and the return of troops from Port Said in December, 1956, Grivas ordered a lull in activities. EOKA regrouped, reorganized, and laid fresh plans for attack.

At the same time, the British security forces were now a more experienced, tougher body, and led by new and able men imported by Harding: Colonel Geoffrey White, an old friend of the governor had been brought in to draw up a report on the antiquated police force, and named chief constable; Colonel White developed good relations with army commanders and helped to solve many of the problems that had hindered their cooperation. A new "Central Intelligence Wing" was formed, in which army and police officers sat side by side, sharing and processing information on every aspect of EOKA. By December this team was working smoothly under a single director of intelligence.

A new military director of operations had also arrived: this was General "Joe" Kendrew who took command of an army of some forty thousand troops which was to score its major successes against the mountain guerrillas.

A year's fighting against the elusive EOKA had taught the British that, as Grivas had put it, a tank was not the best way to catch mice; and several attempts were being made to fight the organization on its own ground, with its own means. Specialized mobile units of Greek and Turkish Cypriots, headed by army interrogators or policemen of the Special Branch worked independently, using their own equipment and transport, free of formal responsibility to superiors who might be alarmed by their methods. The handful of Greek Cypriots who—for whatever reason—had chosen to work for the British, were mainly ruthless men, some with criminal backgrounds. They took leading roles in forceful interrogation: they knew the personal backgrounds of many of the EOKA town and district leaders they were helping to hunt down; and they could make sense of information that would be meaningless to their masters. Thus it was that, by the end of 1956, the British had at last formed a clear intelligence picture of the EOKA organization in mountain and town, and for the first time their commanders in the field were capable of putting that information to good use. It was at the seaport of Limassol that the first major success was scored, with the arrest and breaking up of the arms-smuggling ring at work in the harbor customs office.

Over the past year, EOKA had spent barely one thousand pounds on smuggling some forty boxes of arms to Cyprus. The guns and ammunition cost nothing: they were taken from Greek military stores, with the connivance of senior army officers.

Late in October 1956, following the dispatch of two suitcases filled with guns, Azinas received an urgent warning. Searches in Limassol had given hints that the British were on to something: for four months Special Branch men had been piecing together a picture of the network, and on December 1, they arrested Lefteris Chrysohou, a key figure in the ring.

On December 14, the government announced "the biggest haul of the Emergency"—the arrest of forty-four EOKA members in Limassol, including virtually the entire smuggling ring—receivers, drivers, store-keepers, customs men, and carriers, which included two Limassol school teachers.

It was at this juncture that the British unveiled the constitution which Lord Radcliffe, the jurist, had devised. But the publication of his proposals, on December 19, 1956, made little mark on a situation fraught with strife and mistrust. The horrors of "Black November," the controversy over torture and the continued detention of the Archbishop were not conducive to the calm discussion of a constitution which, while it offered the Greek Cypriots an elected majority in the assembly, made no mention of future self-determination. The control of internal security and foreign affairs was to be retained indefinitely in British hands, and Cyprus would remain under British sovereignty. Makarios was shown the proposals in the Seychelles, but he refused to discuss them while still in exile; and Grivas, in leaflet and in letter to the Greek foreign minister derided the "fake constitution" and warned against attempts to discuss it.

Nor was the political climate improved by the manner in which the Radcliffe constitution was revealed to the House of Commons by the colonial secretary, Alan Lennox-Boyd. For the first time the specter of partition—which had proved so disastrous in Ireland and India—was officially raised by a minister of the crown, Lennox-Boyd suggesting that the Turkish-Cypriot minority, like the Greek-Cypriot majority, should have the right to determine its own future, when the time came for a vote to be taken in the island. The Turkish Cypriots would undoubtedly vote to join Turkey, and Cyprus would then be divided between the Turkish and Greek Cypriots.

In Grivas' view, the constitution was simply a trick which the British were using to divert their critics abroad from the harsh new laws accompanying the latest, most vigorous attempt to suppress EOKA.

At the same time, Turkish Cypriots on the island became increasingly belligerent. Riots followed the death of a Turkish auxiliary policeman in an EOKA bomb attack. A mob looted and burned Greek property, and scores of Greek citizens were assaulted; yet the security forces seemed inert, and twelve hours passed while rioting and arson continued before a curfew was imposed. Greek Cypriot leaders charged that the violence, if not actually instigated by the British, was looked upon by them with some satisfaction and permitted to continue unhindered.

The combined forces of the Turkish-Cypriot underground organization, Volkan, and the Turkish-Cypriot mob, with its calls for blood, proved a valuable weapon in the hands of the Ankara government, which would henceforth call for partition, and nothing less.

At the beginning of 1957, the British dealt a series of punishing blows. The breakup of Limassol's smuggling ring was followed by the arrest of most of the leading gunmen and saboteurs in Nicosia, and eventually of the capital's leadership. Nicos Sampson's team of gunmen and girls was shattered first: following a botched attempt to assassinate a young informer, several of them had been arrested and at least one gunman spoke freely under interrogation. Sampson was identified and a poster with his photograph went up in police stations and army camps everywhere. A captain described him as "the man responsible for killing your friends and innocent civilians."

Sampson moved to Morphou, thirty miles from the capital, but his hunger for action led him to attempt another killing, this time of a Turkish policeman. The attack misfired, and Sampson was wounded in the leg. He was taken to Nicosia for treatment, then to the village of Dhali.

On the following day, Nicosia was cordoned off by some three thousand troops who searched every house and store, street by street. Greek males between the ages of fourteen and forty were shepherded into playgrounds and football fields to be screened in barbed-wire cages known to the military as "playpens." The target of this massive operation was Sampson.

In Sampson's absence, his companions embarked on a further series of shootings. They killed a former member of the Palestine police, in the entrance of his apartment block inside the city walls, then slipped their guns to two schoolgirls, who carried them off in the Kokkinou sisters' latest invention, "the kangaroo skirt"—two deep holster-like pockets stitched into the girls' skirts. They killed three additional Britons, two of them civilians, in similar style in January. But at the end of the month, the British captured a youthful member of the group who had been with Sampson at his Dhali refuge. It did not take interrogators long to make him talk.

Confined to an old village house at Dhali, Nicos Sampson had spent his time gazing at a copy of his own "wanted" poster, which he had pinned to the wall, and writing letters to colleagues in parts of the island where he might once more play an active role. He did not want to take the usual route for hunted men: a passage to the mountains where he would live with other guerrillas in some damp underground cave, perhaps for years.

He was asleep when police and troops, guided to Dhali by the captured youth, burst into the house. He was arrested after a brief struggle and in icy rain was driven back to Nicosia, lying face down, handcuffed and shoeless, in an open truck. Later that night, he signed a confession to a series of murders, including those of the policemen in Ledra Street.

The confession was contested in the courts by Greek-Cypriot lawyers and by Sampson himself, who maintained that it had been extracted by torture. The judge—Justice Bernard Shaw, who had narrowly escaped death at the hands of the gunmen a few weeks previously—rejected this, but excluded the confession on the grounds that Sampson was not in fit condition to make statements to the police after his journey through the rainstorm, and because no medical attention had been given to the numerous minor injuries he had received during his arrest. Without the confession, the prosecution case collapsed.

The acquittal of this most notorious of gunmen, who admitted to at least fifteen slayings, was hailed in Britain as evidence of the rigid propriety, if not the efficacy, of British justices under critical circumstances; however, Sampson was re-tried under a new judge—trial by jury being unknown in Cyprus—and sentenced to death for "attempting to discharge a firearm" at arresting officers.

One after another, key EOKA men in Nicosia fell into the police net: Nicos Koshis, the town's deputy leader; Andreas Rigas and Andreas Houvartas, the "EOKA policemen"; and many lesser figures. The Special Branch worked around the clock, buoyed up by the wave of successes. On February 1, the trail led to the house of Andreas Chartas, the Nicosia leader, and Rita Kallinikou, his chief courier.

The young woman was typing out an order from Grivas, warning the families of informers that they, too, might be punished if they continued to support and assist the "traitors"—when police and troops surrounded the bungalow. While police were breaking down the door, the pair swept up loose EOKA correspondence, rushed to the bathroom and locked themselves in. There they lifted out the false porcelain bidet, set in a slab of concrete, which covered the entrance to the hideout, and shoveled into the hideout papers and false identity cards. Three days earlier this hideout had been filled with weapons, but now there was only a loaded pistol, detonators, and a few sticks of dynamite. As they pushed the bidet back into place, the police knocked on the door with their guns.

Rita Kallinikou opened the door and faced a row of guns in the corridor. The police pushed her into a bedroom as others burst in and dragged out Chartas. In a few minutes they had raised the bidet and revealed the hideout.

In the first nine days of February, EOKA suffered further serious losses. A leader of the courier network was arrested in Nicosia, and from clues in captured EOKA correspondence, together with information from those who had been arrested by the British, police began to suspect that Grivas was hiding somewhere in the Limassol district.

On February 7, searches in the area of the Christodoulides' bungalow in Limassol lasted throughout the day. Grivas and Georghiades could hear soldiers trampling about on the concrete cover of their underground room. But late in the day the operation ended. The elaborate safeguards in Grivas' security system had paid off once more.

— 17 —

Debacle in the Mountains

EOKA's situation in the mountains approached a total rout. Since December 1956 the guerrillas had been on the run from hideout to hideout. British army sweeps were under way, but success came chiefly to the small, aggressive units of police and troops, led by officers who had gained experience of counter-guerrilla work in other colonies. These tightly knit groups lived, worked, ate, and often slept together under rough conditions. Nearly always, they contained a Cypriot informer, a man whose only hope of survival now lay with the British: turned loose to fare for himself in a hostile Cyprus he would almost certainly be murdered; but if he, with his knowledge of the people, language and terrain, could guide them into EOKA, then the British were reliable paymasters. He would live in comfort when not on duty, and in the end be sent abroad with money to spend.

One of the boldest of the specialized mountain patrols was led by Captain Lionel Savery. It was one of their strikes, at the village of Zoopiyi, that turned up information which eventually led to the breakup of every important group in the area. The patrol, backed by a small unit of police and troops, entered the village at midnight. The Cypriot who led them was simply plunging about haphazardly in the dark: he had contacts at one house, but he did not know that Afxentiou, second in rank only to Grivas, was hiding at Zoopiyi with his group. The patrol blocked off one end of a village street while the informer knocked on the door of a house. They lured a village EOKA leader out by saying they had arms that must be hidden. He was pushed into a car for interrogation.

Afxentiou had heard the car arrive, but the patrol was using an old

118

Cypriot taxi as a cover and his suspicions were allayed. However, he sent a man out to reconnoiter and when he failed to return, decided to leave. He and his men walked straight into Savery's patrol. In the ensuing gun battle one EOKA man was killed. Afxentiou, although hit in the leg, escaped with his group.

The mountain operations widened, with helicopters playing a major role, carrying troops from landing grounds at village sports fields to the more inaccessible heights. Time after time, pilots made these journeys, guided by columns of colored smoke, negotiating steep cliff faces whenever a temporary break offered in the winds and driving snow of January.

Afxentiou and his men were meanwhile moving by night from village to village: at Palekhori, a curfew and search forced the group to hide for hours in a tiny hole beneath the house of the village schoolmaster. When curfew lifted they hurried on to Tsericoudi, only to hear more tales of searches and betrayals. They marched on to the monastery of Makheras, where the abbot gave them shelter and food. Days later, a fresh warning came from Grivas, who had information that the monastery was to be searched. Two women couriers, escorted by two policemen in EOKA, raced up to the monastery at nightfall to deliver the message. As they returned, they passed a convoy of army trucks moving uphill to Makheras: Afxentiou had escaped with barely twenty minutes to spare.

But once the army had left Makheras, Afxentiou and his men returned to build a hideout in the nearby hills. A monk brought them supplies and construction materials on muleback, and at a spot known as Jonya, half a mile from the monastery buildings, they widened and strutted a cave in the hillside. Afxentiou split his group into two sections and settled in to wait for news.

It was bad from every side: one three-man group had been betrayed and captured near Yerakies in one of the largest mountain hideouts. This was the first success of "Black Mac," an operation planned by Brigadier Baker, and the biggest yet mounted by Harding; in the next ten weeks twenty-two out of the forty "most wanted" guerrillas would fall into the net.

Now the hunt concentrated on the groups of Markos Drakos, Polycarpos Georgadjis, and Afxentiou. Aware that Drakos was in the area, the army staked out the countryside with scores of small patrols lying in ambush. Large stretches of land had been declared "prohibited areas," where anyone could be, and was, shot on sight. Near Evrykhou village, the guerrillas carrying a heavy Bren gun, passed through a wood. Visibility in the rainy darkness was about three yards. The soldiers lying in wait saw the EOKA leader at the moment he saw them. Drakos gave a shout of warning, and both groups opened fire simultaneously. The guerrillas behind Drakos saw him fall before they ran, bullets whizzing about them; one of them was hit in the leg, but they made an escape through the night, carrying the Bren gun to Kathydas village, where they spent the night. Markos Drakos, struck by thirteen bullets, was dead.

"Operation Black Mac" was deploying impressive forces. Long convoys of British soldiers pulled out of Nicosia with men from a dozen regiments. From Limassol and Platres, support groups headed for the mountains. Searchlights swept the hills and flights of helicopters dropped men at high points throughout the Adelphi forest, despite winds that gusted up to fifty-five knots. Trucks skidded off the icy roads. But eventually the troops were in position, and from mid-January a tight net was thrown around the crucial mountain villages.

As more and more prisoners were questioned, and information was pieced together, so more hideouts were found and blown up, while the remaining groups were pinned down by curfews and searches.

At Omodhos, four miles from British army headquarters at Platres, information led patrols to the house of a Cypriot constable. Paratroopers burst in on a domestic scene: women knitting, an old man reading a newspaper, and two babies swinging in cradles slung from the ceiling. The paratroopers bundled everyone out, doused the fire flaming in the open hearth and prized up a hearthstone: beneath was a hole hardly wider than a man's hips. The guerrillas came out one by one with their hands up. The group leader was the much-sought Polycarpos Georgadjis.

Army commanders called a victorious press conference. General Joseph Kendrew, who had assumed responsibility for all anti-EOKA operations, said that the internal security forces had been reorganized to form one unified force embodying army, RAF, and Cyprus police. The operation was "like a big shoot" to bring out the game birds and "my soldiers are acting as beaters." They still hoped to capture Afxentiou and Grivas, who was thanked "for the wonderful training opportunity afforded the men." [1] More than thirty hideouts had been destroyed, more than sixty guerrillas captured, more than two hundred suspects arrested.

Grivas, for his part, issued a leaflet admitting that "our ranks have been thinned," but promising that the organization would continue its mission: "If everyone stays at his post and does his duty, the wheel will turn in our favor." [2] He attempted to raise popular morale by claiming that the British were concealing their own casualties, and kept up a barrage of leaflets denouncing British "torturers," vandalism by the troops, and brutality in the prisons, which the U.S. consul-general was invited to visit "in order to see the deeds of your allies."

On Februray 15, the guerrilla Stylianos Lenas, rated third on the British "most wanted" list, led a three-man group in the ambush of an army truck on the Amiandos-Saittas road and forced it out of control into a ravine. But two days later Lenas' group blundered into a patrol, and all three fell under a hail of bullets. Lenas, badly wounded, was captured and later died in the hospital. There remained only one major group in the mountains, that of Gregoris Afxentiou.

Afxentiou had converted the cave-hideout near Makheras monastery into a cubicle four feet high, roofed with corrugated iron. The ground was dense with bushes and slippery with shale and rocks. It was not a place easily discoverable by chance, nor could it be approached silently. They trusted Abbot Ireneos, the monastery's director, and in any event there was nowhere left to run: all nearby villages were curfewed and watched, almost every friendly house betrayed. Now a guerrilla, captured at Omodhos, decided to throw in his lot with the British and joined Captain Lionel Savery's patrol. He revealed Afxentiou's presence in the area of the monastery, which the British had recently searched without result. Only Abbot Ireneos and a monk knew the exact location of the hideout; but the informer said that these places inevitably became known to local countrymen: it was simply a matter of finding the right man. Within three days, they found him: a local shepherd, who had taken food to a site near the hideout.

At dawn on March 3, patrols located the hideout, high on the valley's side. The guerrillas heard feet scraping above them. Soldiers began pulling rocks from the entrance. When a shaft of light entered, they heard a British voice calling to them in Greek: "Come out of the hide, leave your arms behind."

Afxentiou told the others to go out. Four men crawled out to face the guns of their captors. But Afxentiou stayed inside, alone. Again the British called on him to surrender, and this time the answer was a burst of automatic fire that killed a soldier. An officer leaped onto the roof of the hideout and tossed in a grenade. There was an explosion, then silence.

The guerrilla Avgoustis Efstathiou shouted, "You've killed him," while the officer took him by the collar and ordered him to bring the body out. But Afxentiou, wounded in the neck, was fully conscious. Efstathiou decided to stay.

"Now we are two," he shouted, and tossed out a grenade.

For the next eight hours, the pair fought back with gunfire and grenade, while the British held repeated conferences on how to root out the two men.

The British had nothing to lose but face, and they were not prepared to risk any more lives. They manhandled three barrels of aviation fuel into position on the slope above the hideout and set a stream of liquid running toward it.

The men inside knew what was coming but still they did not move. The last words Efstathiou heard Afxentiou say was: "Don't be afraid." Then the cave was enveloped in flame. Efstathiou's clothes and hair caught fire and he hurled himself from the entrance, rolling over and over down the hill.

Afxentiou did not come out. The two sides exchanged fire; exploding grenades and ammunition shook the hillside and kept the British at a distance until nightfall. It was not until dawn next day—twenty-four hours after the start of the battle—that Afxentiou's charred corpse was dragged out. One leg had been severed by an exploding grenade, and there was a gaping wound in his head.

Grivas heard the news of the death of his most outstanding lieutenant "with pain and pride." [3] Afxentiou was at once elevated in EOKA literature to the highest place in the pantheon of heroes. But the mountain guerrillas were now destroyed. How had the British achieved, in a matter of weeks, a breakthrough on such a scale? One answer given by Grivas was that the army and police were now working as one, according to a guerrilla strategy of their own. Both in town and countryside EOKA's defense was penetrated by small, highly mobile forces with great resourcefulness and few inhibitions. They had seized the element of surprise and were hoisting EOKA with its own petard. Grivas called especially effective the system of counterambushes used in the mountains against Drakos, Lenas, and others. "We always stood in fear of the lurking cat," he wrote, although he did not agree that the British cat possessed the necessary alertness and stealth to catch the EOKA mice when they re-emerged from hiding. If the security forces finally failed to neutralize EOKA, it was through inadequate preparation and application. The British, he noted, relied heavily on routine; they tried, too often, to employ methods that had succeeded elsewhere, instead of adapting to a new situation.[4]

General Kendrew, who revolutionized EOKA-hunting methods, stated that lessons learned in the guerrilla wars of the Malayan jungles and against the Mau-Mau in Kenya were in fact applied with good results. The old tactic of sending massive forces trudging through perilous country proved of little value.[5]

Much of what had recently been accomplished was the work of six-man teams, each consisting of a leader, a radio operator, two snipers, and two trackers with dogs. But the ultimate key to success was the informer—the "toad," as he was called by soldiers—who often led the way in operations, and who in a few cases played an active role in interrogation, becoming the torturer of his own countrymen.

Some debate on the question of torture had been conducted in British newspapers and in Parliament following the submission of several hundred complaints to the authorities by Cypriot lawyers. These were always rejected as false by the administration in Cyprus, which produced a "White Paper" indignantly denying the allegations. How, it was asked, could your average British policeman, famed the world over for restraint and civility, become a fiend incarnate on reaching Cyprus shores? But the accusations were not leveled at "average" policemen, still less at the "average" national serviceman: the men responsible were a handful of highly trained and experienced experts in counterinsurgency who were sometimes civilians and sometimes of military rank.

Stringent press laws prevented charges of torture from appearing in the Cypriot newspapers, while British reporters on the island, with rare exceptions, avoided the question. It was undoubtedly a propaganda victory for the Cyprus administration: the world at large was persuaded that if torture was indeed occurring, it must be on a minuscule scale. In retrospect, it seems that deliberate ill treatment during interrogation was more common than imagined at the time.

The methods used were primitive, and several Greek Cypriots died in custody. But in no case after 1956 was a legal action successfully brought against an officer, nor was any public investigation worthy of the name made into any of these deaths. A coroner's inquest would be held at which an officer would explain that injuries noted by the government pathologist had been received either in the course of the prisoner's arrest or during a subsequent attempt to escape.

Cypriot lawyers like the highly respected John Clerides, a queen's counsel, protested repeatedly that many of the prisoners they interviewed displayed extensive bruises and contended they were inflicted in custody; but their complaints were either ignored or dismissed as EOKA propaganda. Meanwhile, British newspapermen who raised the issue with the governor were told that an open inquiry—with all its attendant publicity—would only play into EOKA's hands and do more harm than good.

The question moved into the international sphere on February 20, 1957, when Evangelos Averoff, the Greek foreign minister, said during a debate at the United Nations that he had two hundred and thirty-seven signed, handwritten documents from Greek Cypriots who had undergone torture—"horrifying and dreadful" documents, which he would show to the U.N. Secretary General. The British delegate said he should publish them in full or withdraw them. A week later deep uneasiness was expressed in the House of Commons over the methods being employed in Cyprus, but these accusations were met by official denials.

Protests were lodged also against the governor's assumption of power to suppress newspapers without stated reason, and to deprive them of their right of appeal to the courts. These complaints reached a climax when action was taken against the *Times of Cyprus,* which was summoned under the new regulations for "publishing a disturbing report." The article in question, a contribution from a roving correspondent of the London *News Chronicle,* scarcely differed from a hundred other journalistic reports on the temper of the island where, it stated, Sir John Harding was now being criticized by British residents for failing to halt the killings; it went on to speak of the growing demand for vigilante action against the Greek Cypriots.

To defend the *Times of Cyprus,* Sir Frank Soskice a former attorney general of the British Isles under a previous Labour administration arrived from England. His vigorous defense arguing that the Cyprus government's suppression of reports such as those under consideration virtually prohibited all kinds of comment whatsoever on the island's affairs, made no impression on the special justice who presided over the case (there was, of course, no jury). The jurist's verdict, that the article was indeed "likely to be prejudicial to the maintenance of public law and order," was seen as opening the way to full suppression of the *Times* and other newspapers that offered criticism of Harding's administration. And the paper was fined.

Various august organizations came forward on behalf of the *Times of Cyprus* to intercede in the name of press freedom. Fifty Labour and Liberal members of Parliament signed a motion deploring the new laws under which the newspaper ad been fined; the National Union of Journalists and the Commonwealth Press Union called for their abrogation; and the Scottish Liberal party paid the fine "as a mark of its abhorrence of the laws." [6] Faced with this unexpectedly heavy barrage of criticism in Britian, the Cyprus government took no further overt action. In any event, debate on the freedom of the press was temporarily obscured by dramatic developments on the political front.

— 18 —

The Road to Independence

For five days in February 1957, the United Nations debated the question of Cyprus. After refusing to vote on British complaints against Greek support of terrorism and Greek demands for Cypriot self-determination, the Political Committee of the General Assembly adopted a blameless resolution, sponsored by India, calling for negotiations to be resumed in an atmosphere of peace and freedom of expression. On this point, Britain, Greece, and Turkey could agree. The British and Turks, however, foresaw tripartite talks; the Greeks, like the Indians, understood that any negotiations would be Anglo-Cypriot. Since no talks followed, the point was of no lasting significance.

But now Grivas, bowing to repeated urgings from the Greek government, offered to suspend operations if Makarios were released from the Seychelles. On March 14, 1957, Grivas put out leaflets in Cyprus to say that this gesture would be made "in compliance with the spirit of the U.N. resolution and in order to facilitate the resumption of negotiations between Britain and the real representative of the Cyprus people, Archbishop Makarios." It took the British government six days to reply to this offer. The British cabinet was divided; but Harold Macmillan, the new prime minister, who had replaced Sir Anthony Eden after the debacle at Suez, flew back from his first meeting with President Eisenhower in Bermuda to resolve the question: Makarios would be released, although he would not be allowed to return to Cyprus. The immediate result of this decision was the resignation of Lord President of the Council, the Marquess of Salisbury, who had led the hard-line faction within the cabinet. For his part, the Archbishop said that he was not prepared to negotiate about Cyprus unless his return to the island was allowed. It was left to Harding to announce that the security forces had scored a victory, and he renewed his offer of safe conduct for all members of EOKA who wished to leave the island. None did, and no attempt was made to approach Makarios, who had been released and now resided in Athens' Grande Bretagne Hotel.

EOKA, however, was far from being completely destroyed. Its Nicosia organization was leaderless and in disarray, the guerrilla groups had been chased from the mountains; but in other parts of the island EOKA was still largely intact, and Greek Cypriot students offered an ample source of recruits for the groups that Grivas now began to re-form.

A new Nicosia headquarters had to be found—and one unlikely to be subjected to the frequent searches now being conducted in the capital. This was to be in the home of Gabriel A. Gabrielides, a well-to-do Greek businessman and outwardly at least no friend of the EOKA cause. As a prominent member of that British bastion, the Nicosia Club, he liked to invite British friends, including police officers, to his home near the center of the city after the club closed at night. All had curfew passes and often they enjoyed Gabrielides' hospitality in a basement "den" with a well-stocked bar. The festivities sometimes lasted into the early hours of the morning.

It was a brave decision for EOKA to reopen for business in a house frequented by British security officers; yet this was one of the few places in Nicosia assured of freedom from casual raids by the police. Still more daring was the idea of building a hideout in the basement behind the bar. This was suggested by Gabrielides to the first two EOKA men to move into the house—Yannakis Stefanides, who was barely twenty years old, but the ranking member of what was left of the Nicosia command system, and student leader Andreas Nicolaides. Their faith in Gabrielides leaves no question that he was in EOKA's confidence, and was given license to consort with the British for the value of the information he might get from them in their hours of relaxation.

The two young men, assisted by Gabrielides, began to excavate a small room behind the bar along the foundations of the house. Its entrance, a door of thick concrete fastened on the inside by a bolt, was disguised by wall shelves which held rows of bottles. An oxygen cylinder was installed in case long periods of hiding made breathing difficult. Gabrielides daily carried bags of excavated earth out into the countryside in his car and disposed of them.

The work of the two young men was made easier by a relaxation of security which followed the truce declaration. The bishop of Kitium was released from house arrest, curfews were lifted, and some inmates were released from detention camps. Troops flowed back into the towns, and the British army left its requisitioned mountain hotels. But the government made it clear that nothing, in principle, had changed; Harding warned that while Grivas "and his few remaining associates" remained at large, "we cannot afford to lower our guard." [1] This meant that the army could strike at EOKA throughout the truce, while Grivas held his organization back. The longest curfew of the revolt, which lasted fifty-four days, proceeded at Milikouri village, where people were allowed out of their houses only for brief periods, and every house, field, and well was probed for Grivas.

At last the hunt was abandoned, only to recommence a few weeks later in the western half of the island, where Grivas was in his hideout at the home of Marios Christodoulides. This time the British came closer to the prize. Shortly after midnight, on June 6, Grivas and his companions were awakened by the barking of Irma the watchdog, and peering through the shutters, they saw troops and police in the fields outside. A force of more than six hundred men was combing the area. Grivas and Georghiades descended into the hideout and readied their guns and grenades. Marios, having replaced the kitchen oddments on the hideout door, sat down to await the dawn.

When a search party knocked on the door Elli Christodoulides opened it, her baby in her arms. Two soldiers entered and began to search the rooms. Marios, speaking in English, asked if the soldiers would like "a drop of scotch"—his British bank manager had given him a bottle. Soon the visitors and their hosts were gossiping over the glasses. A sergeant arrived and was placated with a double whiskey. Presently they all tramped off, passing over the roof of the hideout. Shortly before noon, Grivas heard the three knocks from the kitchen which meant "all clear" and came from the hideout to learn what had happened.

Apart from such alarms, which arose from the British policy of pursuing what was hoped to be the last remnants of EOKA, the first months of the truce were uneventful. All the revolutionaries awaiting execution were reprieved, but they were flown to the greater security of jails in England to serve their life sentences.

Meanwhile the Turkish-Cypriot militants were not idle. And Grivas heard rumors that members of their underground groups were being trained in Turkey. The British government was giving more serious study to the possibility of partition, and Harding—who had once called it the worst of solutions—returned from talks in London in July 1957 to say that he now considered partition practicable in the sense that it could be achieved. It might be the only solution.

Turkish-Cypriot preparations for counterviolence were revealed in September when a militant group's secret bomb factory was devastated by an explosion. Four men were killed in the blast, and twenty unexploded bombs were found on the scene. For several weeks threatening Turkish leaflets had been appearing without interference by the government, which seemed to accept the Turkish Cypriot leader Dr. Fazil Kuchuk's evaluation of the explosion as "a very unfortunate accident." Plainly, the authorities were not overly disturbed by this evidence of a new Turkish belligerency.

EOKA finally suspended activities on March 31, 1957. And it was seven months later that a new prime minister, Harold Macmillan, took the first step toward pacification. In October he replaced Harding as governor with a professed liberal, Sir Hugh MacKintosh Foot. On Harding's departure, he explained that his successes against the terrorists had opened the way for a civilian administrator. Grivas disagreed. His farewell blast to "the Gauleiter, sadistic murderer and torturer of the Cypriot people" claimed that Harding was leaving the island "humiliated and brought low by a handful of heroes." [2] To vent his displeasure at continuing British military operations and searches, Grivas ordered more sabotage. As a result, the Cyprus Broadcasting Service station was bombed and a magnetic "clam" was smuggled into the hold of a British merchant ship that was loading copper ore; the resulting blast blew a hole below the waterline, but the ship was saved by a repair party from the Royal Navy. Then, on November 26, a young electrician, carrying two bombs in his lunchbox, entered the RAF Akrotiri Air Base, and placed bombs in two Canberra jets. They exploded, igniting fuel tanks. Flames swept through the hangar destroying two more Canberras and a Venom jet fighter.

— 19 —

Breaking the Blockade

The arrival of Archbishop Makarios in Athens had given fresh impetus to Andreas Azinas' efforts to break the arms blockade. Grivas had been urging him to discover a new smuggling route since the arrest of the Limassol customs team in December 1956; and now Makarios' influence could be brought to bear on officials who could supply weapons and facilitate their passage to Cyprus. Makarios also made more money available. But he still kept minute accounts and looked coolly on Azinas' more extravagant plans.

Socrates Eliades, a Nicosia businessman, flew to Athens and discussed with Azinas schemes for importing in refrigerators and fuel tanks electric drills, time pencils, and guns. None of these ideas was realized. And Azinas' next inspiration, by which a powerful speedboat would dash from Athens into Cyprus waters, deposit a load of arms, and return at speed faster than that of any British naval vessel, likewise came to naught. Wild schemes for germ warfare and an invasion by minisubmarines were also abandoned.

Azinas, harassed by Grivas' demands, obstructed by Makarios' caution, and kept under constant surveillance by British agents in Greece, was at his wit's end when, in September 1957, he received a practical suggestion from Cyprus.

After so many failures, a simple but ingenious scheme was devised by Cornelius Kyriakides, a Cypriot postal clerk, who observed that parcels arriving from overseas were not all searched at Limassol, their port of entry. Those for the Paphos district were taken to the remote post office of Ktima, which was supervised by a few British soldiers and Turkish-Cypriot policemen who were supposed to oversee the examination of each parcel as it was handed to the addressee and opened for inspection between eleven o'clock and noon. After the inspection the soldiers departed for the afternoon. What was to stop the Greek-Cypriot workers, asked Kyriakides, from stamping the documents with a forged seal (the one in British hands could easily be copied) and handing out unsearched parcels when the British were absent?

Grivas approved a dummy run, and from Azinas in Athens came a box of Corinthian raisins, bearing special markings and addressed to an imaginary citizen of prearranged nomenclature. The collecting agent was Panayotis Haralambis, a young EOKA member, who simply came to the small side window of the Ktima post office one September afternoon, handed in a slip advising that the parcel was waiting and collected the unchecked box of raisins. (The slip was necessary because the British counted the number of parcels and kept matching counterfoils in a locked safe.) Haralambis was a post office worker who delivered parcels to outlying villages, and he was thus well known to the Turkish-Cypriot policemen on duty at the building who sometimes helped him load his van.

In November 1957 a wooden box labeled "Contents: Almonds" arrived from Athens, addressed to "George Papadopolous, Polis." Haralambis collected it as before while the soldiers were at lunch: the side window shutter popped up, disgorged a wooden box, and clamped down again. The first consignment of guns had arrived. The one remaining policeman was outside, on guard at the main entrance, and did not see the transaction.

Soon two or three boxes were coming in each week. They sat on the post office floor, still in their mailbags, away from British eyes until Haralambis called. The system continued to operate until the end of the rebellion.

In December 1957, a resolution passed in the U.N. General Assembly's Political Committee called for renewed negotiations "with a view to applying the right of self-determination" to Cyprus. The United States abstained from voting in the General Assembly, and her NATO allies followed suit. On the island itself Turkish rioters promptly began to burn and loot Greek-Cypriot shops. Grivas blamed the failure of the negotiations on "the dollar policy" of the Athens government, which he believed to be at the economic mercy of Washington.

The new governor, Sir Hugh Foot, who had been visiting detention camps, city mayors, and other local dignitaries, talking about a new policy that was to come, now flew to Ankara for talks with the Turkish government, which, as always, must be given the first chance to consider the proposals he had drawn up for the future of Cyprus.

The plan provided for the return of Archbishop Makarios to Cyprus and stipulated a period of five to seven years of limited self-government before any final decision as to self-determination was reached. To this the Turks raised "every possible objection," even to the point of threatening to refuse to receive Sir Hugh Foot in Ankara if he proposed also to visit Athens. This rejection, made by telegram to Whitehall, was sufficient to terminate "all our hopes and all our plans," and Sir Hugh "returned to Cyprus with a sick feeling." [1]

The Turks would accept nothing less than partition, and to emphasize the point they instigated from Ankara more and bloodier riots in Cyprus. Back in the island, Sir Hugh broadcast a dramatic appeal for the maintenance of the truce: should EOKA resume violence, he warned, they would "destroy themselves and their cause." A positive moment in this diplomatic fiasco was Sir Hugh's brief meeting in Athens with Makarios in which each man was, if nothing else, able to take the measure of the other.

With the "Foot Plan" aborted by Turkey, Grivas warned on March 6, 1958, that the new governor's "credit of time" had run out and that "the fight must go on." There followed a series of explosions in power stations, military camps, and at the new police headquarters, then being built at a cost of 3 million pounds. No action was taken without Grivas' direct order until March 31, when he passed the initiative to section leaders, allowing them to attack any target so long as no danger to human life was involved.

At the same time he ordered an economic boycott: Cypriots were forbidden to purchase British drinks, confectionery, shoes, cigarettes, soap, clothing, cars, cosmetics, furniture, canned food. Football pools and other forms of gambling were barred.

Disobedience was punished. Masked men walked into cafes and clubs to denounce merchants before the crowd for dealing in British products. Small shopkeepers who persisted in selling British goods were named and warned in EOKA's leaflets. For a first offense they might be told to close for a number of days; for a second they could be fined or totally boycotted. One victim of this system was Grivas' own niece, Lili Gregoriou, a young widow with a small child, who ran a shoeshop in Nicosia. The major Greek Cypriot business interests, all closely involved with Britain, protested privately, but there was little they could do. EOKA spies at the docks informed on any imports of prohibited goods.

Grivas also continued to stir up the prisons and camps. On April 1, 1958—anniversary of the revolution's start—he ordered a general strike, which was followed by a fortnight of disturbances. On April 10 there were simultaneous outbreaks at Camp K, the detention center, on the plain outside Nicosia, and at the central prison; in the capital itself, crowds marched on Government House to protest the continuance of detention without trial. At Camp K the British army was called in to restore order, and stayed on to run the camp on the lines of a military prison.

Grivas immediately issued a leaflet warning Foot that "if ill-treatment and torture of arrested persons and detainees continues I shall order attacks against the British. You bear full responsibility for the mediaeval and dishonest methods used by the inquisitor-torturers of the intelligence service." [2]

Four days later William Henry Dear, a Special Branch interrogator, was killed by two Greek Cypriot youths in a Famagusta street. Police said that one youth had been identified as a projectionist at the Heraon Cinema, a few yards from the scene of the shooting. That afternoon police announced that ten bombs had been found in a hideout behind the projection room. They were "too dangerous to move" and must be detonated on the spot. The cinema manager's plea to be allowed to remove them himself was refused. At sundown, a police siren wailed a warning over the city and two minutes later the cinema dissolved in an explosion that snapped telegraph poles and hurled debris for hundreds of yards. Such portions of the building as remained standing were seized by the authorities, who refused all compensation to the Cypriot owners; to the owners such action was merely a new twist to more legal forms of mass punishment. The military vigorously denied that they were carrying out reprisals of their own.

— 20 —

Split Between Grivas and Makarios

Sir Hugh Foot, alarmed by the deteriorating situation, attempted to make direct contact with Grivas, in the hope of persuading him against continued violence. To this end, he called to Government House Glafkos Clerides, a leading lawyer, to ask his help in sending a letter to Grivas. It would be written in his own hand, and none but the two of them and Grivas would know of its existence. The letter warned that the campaign of sabotage was leading the people of Cyprus toward disaster. "If it would help," wrote the governor, "I am prepared to go to any place at any time you nominate to meet you and urge you to act on this call. I would come alone and unarmed and would give you my word that for that day you would be in no danger of arrest." [1]

Grivas thought the letter was a trap. He did not believe that Foot would act thus without the approval of his government. As for halting the sabotage campaign, that too was a trick; he believed that Foot wanted time to plot. Yet an outright refusal of such an appeal would be used against EOKA. After long thought, Grivas compromised. He ordered sabotage to cease and simultaneously issued a leaflet on April 21:

> Before I order a general attack I consider it my duty to appeal to the British Government to take the initiative in beginning negotiations for a solution of the Cyprus problem. . . . I am simply giving a warning. As a humane person, I wish to avoid more bloodshed. . . . As Leader, however, I intend to obey the voice of Cyprus, which commands that I liberate her, or fall. [2]

There had been over fifty acts of sabotage in the past week, but beginning with April 21, EOKA was quiet.

134

The British army knew nothing of this secret diplomacy. It continued its widespread searches, and Cypriot workers were dismissed from jobs in military camps. Disturbances by the Cypriot inmates of Camp K were sharply suppressed.

Grivas issued another leaflet warning "Governor Foot": "I give you two days' notice that unless all measures against political prisoners cease, I shall strike back at the British in reprisal." [3] Grivas did not wait for improvement in the situation at Camp K. He felt now that he had allowed Foot's dramatic appeal to draw him off course, and he regretted stopping the sabotage. On April 28, declaring that there was no sign that ill-treatment of political prisoners had stopped, he ordered reprisals against British soldiers.

On Sunday morning, May 4, two young soldiers wearing civilian clothes and carrying pistols were patrolling Famagusta, when two gunmen stepped from a doorway and shot both soldiers in the back.

In the curfew and search operation that followed more than seven hundred youths were arrested. At one British army camp angry troops made people run a gauntlet of blows. About one hundred Cypriots were treated on release for bruises and minor injuries. But neither of the two gunmen was found.

That night Sir Hugh Foot reimposed emergency regulations, including the mandatory death penalty for carrying arms, which had been repealed by Harding. An official statement praised the troops in Famagusta for acting with "commendable restraint, having regard to the brutal murder of their comrades."

The governor flew to London for talks with the British cabinet, as Grivas issued a new warning: "The black November of 1956 will seem pale grey compared to what will happen if the British Government tries to impose a solution to its own liking . . . in opposition to self-determination." [4]

Grivas was now ready to begin again full-scale operations. Arms were flowing in through Paphos, guerrilla bands were forming in the mountains, new leaders had built up groups in all towns and had created reserves of homemade explosive. But he was not sure that he could continue to direct the organization from Limassol; Nicosia would be more satisfactory for many reasons, and no more dangerous. The first necessity was a house with a hideout, in the capital.

The Kokkinou sisters, once more in charge of the courier network, were told to find a means of transporting Antonis Georghiades, Grivas' aide, from Limassol to Nicosia. They decided to use a Shell Oil Company tank truck which made regular journeys carrying gas from the Limassol docks and which had been put at their disposal by Loulla Kokkinou's brother-in-law, who was head of the island's biggest transport company.

Loulla inspected the truck. It would be a simple matter for Georghiades to clamber up the steel ladder at the rear of the vehicle, walk along the gangway and lower himself into one of the truck's three empty compartments, then screw the cover down. Dipstick and valve hole provided air, and a detergent wash dispelled the fumes of gas.

All went smoothly on Georghiades' trip to Nicosia. He met the truck as arranged a few hundred yards from the Christodoulides' house in Limassol and, with Loulla and Ourania leading the way in their car, traveled in two hours to the capital. With the help of Deacon Anthimos Kyriakides, an EOKA agent, he found a new bungalow which seemed suitable for a hideout in a quiet area behind the city's Armenian cemetery. To live in the house, he chose Andreas Lambrou, a young dentist who was earmarked to take over the chief courier's job in case of emergency. Lambrou was single, and lived with his widowed mother. He bought the house with money supplied by the Church and, under Georghiades' direction, started work on a hideout identical in all respects, down to the entrance through a kitchen cupboard, to that in Limassol. Georghiades, Lambrou, and others helped with the digging, but it was Lambrou's mother, a peasant from Panayia, birthplace of the Archbishop, who did most of the work. She heaved the sacks of earth out on her shoulders, brushing aside Georghiades' offers of assistance.

Georghiades visited the Greek consul, the bishop of Kitium, and others, delivering Grivas' latest missives; he was driven by Niki Kyriakides, the deacon's wife, a young woman who had at one time served in the British army. She knew English ways and was confident of her ability to charm her way out of tight corners.

Georghiades' face and name appeared in the booklet, Wanted Men, carried by patrols, but the picture was a poor one; and as Niki Kyriakides remarked, he might almost pass for an Englishman himself, with his blue eyes and fair hair. He stayed with the Lambrous at their Nicosia home adjoining the dental surgery. The windows looked down on Ledra Street—"murder mile," the most heavily policed area of the capital, a noisy race of cars, lorries, and schoolchildren on bicycles, their chatter mingling with the cries of beggars in wheelchairs made from orange boxes.

On a visit to the Gabrielides' home, Georghiades met Polycarpos Georgadjis, who had recently escaped from the Nicosia prison by concealing himself under a pile of garbage in a trash-collection truck. Now he was leader in the capital again, and was living with the two young men who had first sought refuge in the Gabrielides' home—Stefanides and Nicolaides; together they were constructing a series of hideouts in "safe houses" around town. One was known as "the Embassy hideout" because of its proximity to the new block that housed the United States consulate-general. The hideout was in a secret compartment of the loft; two adjoining small cellars were packed with arms. Perhaps due to the nearness of the consulate and the large American flag which flew each day on the grounds, the house had never been searched during the struggle and it was, as Georgadjis remarked, "the one place where we feel safe enough to sit in the garden."

In May Georghiades met the consul at Deacon Anthimos Kyriakides' apartment and was briefed on what the Athens government knew of current talks in London: it appeared that yet another plan for limited self-government would soon be unveiled. Georghiades returned by the tank truck to Limassol with a long report for Grivas.

A few miles north of Limassol, among the vineyards of Mathy-koloni, another major search for Grivas was under way. Some two thousand troops led by tracker dogs were deployed in "Operation Kingfisher," described as the biggest manhunt of the fourteen-month-old truce. Grivas heard from his agents that the British were more than usually confident: that they had information of his presence in the Limassol area seemed plain; and early one May morning the Christodoulides' household received another visit from an army patrol.

Irma the dog had died, and this seriously weakened Grivas' defenses. None of the succession of mongrels brought home by Marios had Irma's intelligence or bravery. Some had barked so often that Grivas was kept in a constant state of alarm; others barked so rarely that he found himself typing busily behind the closed shutters while troops wandered in the garden a few feet away.

Elli Christodoulides was now eight months pregnant, and her small daughter Miria demanded much of her attention. Thus it happened that the household was startled one morning by a knock on the door, shortly after Marios had left for work and while Georghiades was still in the bath. Grivas peered through the shutters and saw British uniforms. He rushed to the kitchen and dropped into the hole under the sink, with Georghiades, a towel draped round his waist, after him. Elli ran to the bathroom and donned a bathrobe and a shower cap. Soldiers were rapping noisily on the door as she padded in bare feet to open it.

The patrol was led by a corporal who, embarrassed at interrupting a woman in her bath, gave the four small rooms of the house only a cursory glance. Elli watched them move off down the road before sounding the ''all clear''—three raps on the hideout cover.

As his sixtieth birthday approached, on May 23, Grivas was occupied with two increasingly troublesome elements of the situation: the British exploitation of the conflict between Greeks and Turks; and his personal conflict with Makarios over the campaign of passive resistance.

The economic boycott, ordered by Grivas, was to him a form of *de facto* Enosis: it was his brainchild, and there was a purity in the notion that one must eat Greek, smoke Greek, talk Greek, and buy Greek that sounded a deep chord in his fanatical nature. Let the people, as he had, put away their foreign fleshpots, don suits of homespun gray, and realize their true Greek natures.

Some of the people agreed, but generally they were unable to respond wholeheartedly, especially when EOKA began to enforce the boycott with acts of violence. The windows of offending merchants were smashed, shopkeepers were beaten by gangs of youths, women who wore imported British dresses had them stripped from their backs in public, or had their heads shaved. Street signs bearing English names vanished under blue paint, and the Turks retaliated by obliterating Greek names and signs with daubs of red. Sometimes EOKA executioners enforced with guns the prohibition against gambling, charging that Cypriots who lost their money at dice or cards were tempted to accept British bribes. The businessmen complained to Makarios in Athens about the boycott, but when the Archbishop suggested to Grivas certain relaxations, and hinted that it might be doing more harm than good, Grivas was incensed. He wrote on April 28, 1958:

> Allow me to express my amazement at what you say about the progress and results of passive resistance. Your informants have been in touch only with the dissatisfied rich, who have seen a small portion of their profits, made from the sweat of the people, drained away. These are certainly the same people who have been nibbling away at the brains of the

Consul and the Bishop of Kitium. . . . The poor, the workers, the peasants, have given their blood and money while the rich sat back and applauded. Now these sharks are asked to make some negligible sacrifices. . . . This is the limit. . . . I must pause in the path I have hacked out, and consider. The way ahead is divided and I am considering my road. . . .[5]

When Makarios later returned to the subject, and even expressed displeasure over Grivas' handling of the Turkish-Cypriot threat, Grivas exploded with rage. He refused to reply to the Archbishop directly and informed the deputy ethnarch, Bishop Anthimos, that he doubted Makarios' fitness to lead the struggle: if his present attitude persisted, Grivas would "no longer give him carte blanche to express the opinion of, or represent the organization." [6] A rift had opened in the EOKA ranks which would never quite be closed, and it could scarcely have happened at a less opportune moment.

— 21 —

Civil War

Three months of planning and discussion in London and Nicosia had resulted in another British initiative, the "Macmillan plan," which reflected Britain's changed view of her strategic requirements in the Middle East after the Suez debacle. After so many years of insistence on the need for Cyprus as a base, the government in London now said that it wanted only a base on Cyprus. No longer was the intervention of foreign powers rejected; instead, the governments of Greece and Turkey were invited to send representatives to sit with the governor and six Cypriot ministers on a council which would rule the island. As ever, the British reserved matters of defense and internal security to themselves, but there would be separate Greek and Turkish Houses of Representatives, and after seven years the situation would be reconsidered.[1]

This plan was to be formally unveiled in the British Parliament on June 19, 1958, but the Turks, insistent on partition, did not wait. There were rumors of a Turkish invasion of Cyprus, which caused NATO to ask the British to postpone announcement of the scheme. Macmillan agreed, but to little purpose.

On the night of June 7 a bomb was detonated on the steps of the Turkish Information Office in Nicosia: it was the signal for simultaneous riots in the Cypriot capital and in Istanbul, where Greek-owned shops and homes were looted and burned, and citizens of the large Greek minority beaten to death. In his memoirs, Foot wrote:

> I was woken in the middle of the night to see from the balcony of Government House what looked like the whole of Nicosia aflame. There followed two months of what we had always most feared, civil war between the Greek and Turkish communities. . . .[2]

140

Entire streets of shops were looted by the Turkish-Cypriot mob, then burned to the ground. The failure of British troops to intervene for some hours was attributed by the Greeks to a deliberate policy. Foot replied that the troops' magnificent work had in fact prevented slaughter on a vaster scale.

Grivas restrained EOKA, believing that the British were in collusion with the Turks in a plot to make him show his strength and "draw his fire." He could see no point in fighting a war on two fronts which might weaken Greek resistance and prove Ankara's claim that "Greek and Turk could no longer live together." But to Makarios in Athens, EOKA's inaction was reprehensible and discouraging to the embattled people. His complaints to associates soon reached Grivas' ears—as they were doubtless intended to do—inspiring a tantrum on his part. He would not be drawn along by events, he wrote to the Archbishop on June 26. The British had set a trap to make him expose his forces at full strength so that they might deal a fatal blow.

The communal conflict spread rapidly throughout the island. The Turkish attacks were of an extravagant ferocity. A mother-superior was murdered at the gates of her convent; a shepherd boy of eleven was found with his throat cut. And on the afternoon of June 12, at the Turkish village of Geunyeli near Nicosia, there occurred a massacre which to Greeks appeared to confirm EOKA charges of Anglo-Turkish collusion. A British patrol arrested thirty-five Greek villagers who had armed themselves with sticks and clubs in self-defense against a rumored attack. They were to be brought to Nicosia and formally charged with carrying weapons, but because of trouble in the city they were taken to a point on the road thirteen miles from their home villages and told to walk home. A band of Turkish Cypriots armed with axes and butcher's knives fell on them, killing nine men and severely wounding five others. Limbs were hacked from bodies, one victim was decapitated, and a wave of horror passed through an island long accustomed to atrocities perpetrated during centuries of Turkish occupation.

The governor ordered an inquiry under the supervision of Chief Justice Sir Paget Bourke, which eventually found that "all concerned acted in the belief that once the prisoners were on their way across country leaving Geunyeli . . . they ran no risk or danger. There was no intention to make these people, so to speak, run the gauntlet. . . ." [3] Nine Turkish Cypriots were later tried for these killings and acquitted.

EOKA was quick to denounce this "new conspiracy" by "Mr. Foot

and his blood-drenched assassins''; but it was not until the end of the
month that the civil population had been organized into "defense
teams" capable of repelling Turkish-Cypriot attacks, nor until July 9
that Grivas removed all restrictions on killing Turks, whether in self-
defense or in reprisal. The result was a sharp increase in isolated shootings which brought the death toll to fifty-six Greeks and fifty-three
Turks murdered before the civil strife ended in early August, as suddenly as it had begun.

In response to a joint appeal for peace from the premiers of Britain,
Greece, and Turkey, Grivas called a new cease-fire on August 4; and
the Turkish Cypriots, whose belligerency had dwindled in the face of
armed resistance, followed suit two days later, when TMT, their underground organization, issued a leaflet announcing a suspension of activity.

The British forces had been placed in a curious position by the civil
war: in attempting to defend Greeks against Turkish onslaughts, they
found themselves aligned with EOKA, whose destruction was their
prime objective. Yet, even at the height of the intercommunal strife,
troops were drawn into conflict with Greek civilians over such minor
matters as painted slogans. On July 5, 1958, four armored cars entered
the small village of Avgorou, near Famagusta and attempted to remove
a banner, stretched across a street, which bore the single word
"EOKA." A boy instructed to pull down this object was seized and
protected by village women; soldiers were attacked with stones; rein-
forcements were summoned and in minutes the square was a melee of
battling men and women. Bicycles, steel stakes, bottles of beer, and
rocks were hurled at the invaders. Then an officer fired a 15-round burst
from a machine gun mounted in the turret of his scout car. The crowd
scattered, leaving two dead bodies in the square. A farmer had been
shot through the chest and the skull of a young woman, the mother of
six, shattered by a shell.

In Famagusta, a few days later, two soldiers were killed by EOKA
gunmen. One was the son of a British peer, the other, a trooper in the
Royal Horse Guards; they were ordering groceries for their regiment
when two young Greeks burst into the store and shot them.

The killers fled the scene on bicycles and hid their guns in the spare
tire of a car two miles away before curfew and search operations began.
When troops arrived they focused on the Anorthosis Sports Club, op-
posite the grocery where the murders had been committed. There they

discovered grenades, mortar shells, and other explosives, which they claimed were "in dangerous condition" beneath the floor of the billiards room and—as in the case of the Heraeon Cinema—they must be blown up *in situ*. The British commander, General Kendrew, presided at the scene and rejected the pleas of Cypriot owners who offered to remove the explosives themselves. Bomb disposal experts wired the cache and detonated it in the evening, destroying the building.

Incident followed upon incident: troops opened fire on a riotous crowd at Akhyritou village, not far from Avgorou, killing a blind man and a boy. This time the victims of EOKA's reprisal were an army colonel, killed by gunmen in the garden of his Limassol home; and a British sergeant, assassinated in a Nicosia street, while walking with his small son. The bloodshed continued against a background of emotional propaganda from both sides. While the Cyprus Broadcasting Service raised its voice against "these most brutal and cowardly murders" and dwelt at length on stories that Greek bystanders had refused to help the dying men, EOKA leaflets thundered threats against "the murderers of children."

Foot now had resort to other methods used by his predecessor: he declared a two-day "standstill," banning all movement on the roads and curfewing every town in the island while the most massive round-up of suspects the island had yet seen was carried out. Some 1500 Greek Cypriots were arrested in an operation that exceeded anything attempted against the civil population by Harding. Two new detention camps were waiting to house them.

Harold Macmillan decided in August 1958 to visit the island and call on his counterparts in Athens and Ankara to discuss the latest British plan for self-government under the joint aegis of Britain, Greece, and Turkey—a policy which he declared himself determined to impose on Cyprus whatever the opposition of the other parties concerned.

The British premier's apparently baseless optimism was, in fact, well grounded: the Turkish government was about to have a change of heart which would bring it full circle from violent opposition to full support of the "Macmillan Plan." [4] For this, he had apparently to thank the United States which, alarmed both by a withdrawal of Greek forces from the NATO headquarters at Izmir in protest at Turkish actions and by the revolution of July 1958 that placed Iraq in Communist hands and virtually destroyed the Baghdad Pact, had reinforced its standing in Turkey with a loan of $359 million and a further accommodation

regarding existing debts of some $800 million. Following the announce-
ment of this economic grant, and the visit of Macmillan in early August,
the Turkish premier, Adnan Menderes, declared that he would cooperate
with the British in implementing the plan and dispatch a Turkish representative to the island on October 1, 1958, the date appointed by Britain.

Faced with a drift toward a possibly disastrous *fait accompli,* Archbishop Makarios felt obliged to modify his demands and abandon, temporarily, the call for Enosis. In its place he had sketched out a scheme
for an independent Cyprus Republic, with the support of the Greek government, and this he was now ready to unveil. His manner of doing so
was, perhaps, unfortunate.

On a visit to Greece and Cyprus at that time was Mrs. Barbara Castle,
a minister in the Labour party's shadow cabinet, whose suggestion that
British troops, while engaged in searches for the killers after a shooting,
were permitted to use unnecessarily rough measure, had caused considerable outrage in Britain. As a former left-wing journalist and a critic of
the military, she was not perhaps the ideal person to interpret the Archbishop's proposal to the Colonial Office in London; but it was to her
that Makarios, through an interview, revealed his plan.

Her attempts to explain the idea in Britain were obscured by the furor
over her comments on the behavior of the troops, made at a time when a
general election was only months away. The leaders of her party were
unprepared to risk giving further offense to public opinion.

One week later, on September 28, 1958, the Archbishop's new proposals were submitted formally to the Colonial Office by Spyros Ky-
prianou, the Cyprus ethnarchy's London representative—and were rejected within two days.

The Archbishop's concession, after four years of obstinate struggle
for union with Greece, astonished most Cypriots, and not least Grivas,
who had not been consulted and was disinclined to believe what he read
in the press of an interview with Mrs. Castle; but on September 28, he
received a letter from Makarios to say that it was correct: independence,
not self-determination would be the battle cry at the coming debate in
the United Nations. The Archbishop could see no other way out of the
impasse: the "imposition" of the Macmillan Plan meant simply that the
Turks would be brought into the island's government and given rights
which later might prove impossible to withdraw. It seemed that British
public opinion was now so inflamed that the Labour opposition could do

nothing unless some new initiative was offered from the Cypriot side; while the United States was supporting Prime Minister Macmillan's efforts, thus necessitating a change of Greek strategy at the U.N. if progress was to be made.

Grivas had planned a new guerrilla offensive to counter the first phase of the Macmillan Plan. On September 25, he gave group leaders free rein to attack their chosen targets at will until the end of November, when the Cyprus question again came before the General Assembly's Political Committee. The prospects for peace seemed darker than ever before. Yet the fighting in Cyprus had in fact barely two months left to run.

— 22 —

Counter-terror

As October approached, amid warnings of imminent "disaster" from King Paul of Greece and his ministers, tension in the island sharply increased. The Archbishop declared that the introduction of the Macmillan Plan would end all hopes of reaching a solution, and EOKA leaflets struck a note of deepening vengefulness.

In the city of Famagusta, especially, feelings were raw and bruised by reprisal and counter-reprisal. Leaflets which purported to come from British vigilante organizations, bearing names like AKOE (EOKA spelled backward) and "Cromwell," were thrown in the streets, urging Britons to "strike back mercilessly" at Greek Cypriots, to "buy British," and to introduce military courts. A long summer of bloodshed and rising hysteria had darkened the mood of troops who, with a few exceptions, had been restrained by traditional disciplines until this moment. The new mood was reflected in the British press which called for stronger measures against the gunmen and spoke openly of the use of torture in interrogation.

Yet some semblance of civilized life remained in Famagusta, Shakespeare's mellow "seaport in Cyprus" which boasted among its attractions the "tower of Othello" set in the old city's Venetian walls. British families still swam from the beaches, though under the protective muzzles of machine guns and separated from Cypriots by barbed wire. Army wives still pushed baby carriages through the heavily patrolled streets. When no curfew obtained, the open air cinemas were filled with people. One night two youths followed an informer into a theater showing "Davy Crockett," and shot him three times through the back.

On October 1, as Makarios called for "vigorous opposition" to the plan and the island lay silent under a general strike, a crowd of demonstrators marched through Famagusta, shouting slogans and blocking roads with oil drum barriers. Troops made a baton charge and were repelled by stones. An army truck tried to ram the barrier, but overturned and burst into flames. Bombs were hurled from a nearby rooftop and soldiers opened fire, wounding a Cypriot. Massive searches began, the doors of private residences were forced, and people were dragged into the streets by enraged troops.

Next day violence burst out in every part of the island. A radio engineer—the first British civilian to die in eighteen months—was murdered by gunmen in a Larnaca street; and in Nicosia, a United States vice consul was shot in the garden of his home by youths who made off on a motorscooter. Despite four bullets in the back, he survived.

Braving these dangers, two British women ventured out on October 3 into Famagusta, to shop for clothes. Until this moment, although Englishwomen had died as a result of EOKA action, none had been deliberately assassinated. But the "execution squads" in Famagusta now had new instructions. After October 1 they might kill any English person, man or woman. Local section leaders passed on the word from the Famagusta commander, who took his directives from Grivas: "The order is an eye for an eye." The British had killed a Cypriot mother of six children at Avgorou. Nor was she the first to die: EOKA had issued a leaflet naming eighteen Cypriot women and children allegedly shot on the island in similar incidents.

At four in the afternoon, as the city was reviving from the siesta hour, two gunmen sat waiting and watching in a shop on Hermes Street. One, who had already played a role in previous executions, carried an automatic pistol in his belt beneath a loose shirt; for the second, this would be a first assassination. They had sought a target for three days without success; and they were about to abandon the attempt when three Englishwomen entered a small dress shop across the street.

One of the women, the wife of an army sergeant, was accompanied by the oldest of her five children, and by another army wife. Few people were in the street as they emerged, after some minutes, from the shop. The gunmen fell into step behind them. On a word from the leader, they pulled out their weapons and shot the women in the back. The two women fell, struck by several bullets; but the girl ran behind a car. She saw the two gunmen run down the narrow street.

One of the women died almost immediately. A Greek Cypriot pharmacist gave first aid to the other, while all around them the steel shutters of shops crashed down as people fled the area before a curfew and search operation began. Police found the dead woman's body sprawled face down in the road; the other woman lay conscious, but bleeding profusely.

Troops from four regiments were rushed to the town to begin the roundup of every Greek male over the age of fourteen. The governor, alerted in Nicosia, "knew that it would be impossible to hold our troops." He summoned General Kendrew and left at once for Famagusta, "but already the troops had gone wild . . . hundreds of Greeks were being treated for wounds inflicted indiscriminately by the furious soldiers." [1] In the streets near the scene of the killing, car windows were smashed with rifle butts, doors broken open and men dragged into the street. Some were driven along at a run, others kicked or thrown bodily into waiting trucks. All over the city, cars were stopped and their owners hustled off. A youth who tried to run was brought down by a bullet through the shoulder. A young girl ran home from school in a state of terror and there died of a heart attack. One man was pulled from the bed where he lay ill and literally kicked outside to a truck. He was buried under a pile of bodies, fracturing seven ribs, and died of "heart failure accelerated by respiratory embarrassment." [2] A young student was driven to an army camp and, like scores of others, made to run a gauntlet of kicks, blows, and punches delivered by some three hundred men of the regiment to which the husband of the murdered woman belonged. He died some hours later, from a skull fracture.

In the beams of truck headlights, Cypriots were "screened" in barbed wire pens, then released in a process that went on until late that night. Some two hundred and fifty went to local hospitals and clinics for treatment; three had died as a direct result of the debacle. But "it was a wonder that there were not far worse casualties that afternoon," noted Sir Hugh Foot, whose prompt appearance on the scene with Kendrew possibly helped to avert a greater tragedy.

Later that night there was looting in the shattered shops. Cameras, watches and similar articles were stolen by soldiers. But the edge of anger was blunted, and now the stage was given over to reproach and recrimination. It was announced that the wounded woman was expected to live; and next day all but two of some four thousand arrested Cypriots were released.

The Greek government realized that it was losing its last British allies: those few Labour politicians who had murmured in support of Barbara Castle's charges were now effectively silenced by the murder of the Englishwoman; and the United Nations debate lay only weeks ahead. Averoff, the foreign minister, met with Makarios to seek ways of repairing the damage; then he wrote to Grivas urging him, whatever had happened, to denounce the crime. Without waiting for a reply, Averoff declared that Greek Cypriots could "never" be responsible for what had happened.

On receiving Averoff's message, Grivas—though highly indignant over the foreign minister's supposed failure to condemn the British reprisal or to mention the deaths of Greek women—issued a reluctant statement which sought to place the blame elsewhere:

> On the pretext that EOKA has murdered two Englishmen, four regiments rush on Famagusta to arrest the murderers. This shows that all was premeditated and prepared. How did it come about that four regiments surrounded the town in a split second as if military operations were on? We ask, though we are sure they will not answer: WHO KILLED THE ENGLISHWOMEN? [3]

The Archbishop made a statement at the same time, carrying a similar implication. The Englishwoman's blood had been spilled not by Cypriots but by "other suspicious and dishonest hands." In Cyprus, the rumor mongers explained that the hands in question belonged to British agents, for who but the British stood to profit from an act so damaging to the national cause?

The killers themselves were meanwhile hiding in the orange groves north of Famagusta. Here they buried the guns in glass jars (covered with rubber to baffle detection devices), and changed their shirts in case the color had been noted. They were never caught and both still live in Cyprus. One became an officer in the Cyprus army.

Grivas formally denied that he ever ordered an attack on a woman, but he did not, in his *Memoirs*, rule out the "possibility of a misunderstanding"; and it seems most charitable to suppose that some ambiguity in the wording of an order resulted in the killing by—as he put it—"a hot-headed Greek seeking to revenge the frequent attacks on the women of our community." [4]

Grivas had no intention of diminishing his campaign because of the uproar about the murdered woman. On October 7, he ordered the guerrilla groups to attack whatever targets offered, to join the already active killer and sabotage teams in a general onslaught on all fronts. Two Royal Air Force jet aircraft were blown up on the runways of carefully guarded bases, roads were mined, and army trucks bringing in relief troops, were blown up, with great loss of life. Scores of events like these assured Cypriots that EOKA was once more in command of the situation. In the three weeks following "imposition" of the Macmillan Plan, the organization mounted fifty ambushes: twenty-five people were killed and more than three hundred injured.

General Kendrew was now leaving the island at the end of his tour of duty, to be replaced by a new director of operations. This was Lt. General Kenneth Darling who had fought alongside General Massu of Algeria in the Suez conflict, and had no hesitation in characterizing EOKA members, as "bastards," "thugs," and "seventeen-year-old louts."

Describing his new methods in a newspaper interview,[5] Darling said that they were based on the realization that EOKA now had mass support and that to suppress this would require the kind of force used by the Russians in Hungary. The Darling plan assumed that every Greek was a possible EOKA supporter and every home a potential store of arms. The capture of couriers was vital: their written messages could unravel a series of threads which led to EOKA's center. Thus his army would work with more stealth: it would take its boots off, for a start. Soldiers in soft shoes stole in threes or fours along darkened streets, lurked in doorways, and sometimes broke into apartments and hotel rooms to search for the elusive terrorists. In the countryside, too, new tactics were employed: soldiers with faces daubed with red paint to simulate blood were made to lie in forest paths, their weapons placed close beside them, while other troops waited in ambush to seize anyone who approached. Still other servicemen were sent out into the mountains on mules, to act as bait to draw EOKA from its hiding places. No spectacular successes were reported.

British civilians were offered training in the use of small arms, and housewives were permitted to shop only in restricted hours, under the eyes of armed troops in bulletproof jackets. Sir Hugh Foot felt constrained to reintroduce more repressive "emergency regulations," including those that created special "danger areas," where soldiers could shoot on sight anything that moved. Sabotage by Cypriot workers inside the military camps culminated in a bomb explosion at an army canteen which killed two men and mutilated others. As a consequence, the governor barred more than five thousand Greek-Cypriot workers from all military establishments. To replace them in canteens and kitchens, several hundred Englishmen and women were flown out from Britain.

This tense and emotional situation was plainly wearing down British restraint: the cumulative anger of the years was boiling over into vigilante action and reprisals.

The Peace Conference

Little was expected of the United Nations debate in December 1958, and it seemed that years of fighting might lie ahead. For some time, Grivas had been urging his associates in Athens to find a safe and speedy way to supplement EOKA's arsenal. And now Andreas Azinas and his team worked out a plan.

Cyprus maintained no piped gas supply: the vast majority of homes used cylinders of gas imported by the thousands from Italy and Greece; and it occurred to Azinas that here was a perfect way to trick the customs. At the Nicosia end of the smuggling line was Socrates Eliades, the Nicosia businessman who had both transport and a trusted staff. He could work out a deal with local agents of the Kosangas Company, one of the importers.

It was found that each cylinder could hold two M3 automatics with magazines or four revolvers with ammunition. By replacing the heavy liquid gas within the cylinders by a slight charge of gas, the weight of these weapons would be neutralized. The difficult part of the job, however, would be to open the cylinders, fix the guns firmly inside and reseal them in total secrecy. Throughout November 1958, Azinas, his fiancee Maroulla and four helpers worked day and night in their Athens workshop emptying the cylinders, slicing away the base of each with a steel saw, and welding the guns inside with copper wire to prevent movement. Trickiest of all was the welding of boxes of ammunition directly to the base of the cylinders. Azinas operated the oxy-acetylene lamp while Maroulla threw water over the red hot joints. The risk of an explosion was great, the work hot and exhausting. But at last it was done. At Piraeus, the port of Athens, Azinas sat watching as one hundred cylinders, containing sixty automatic weapons, forty-five pistols, and seventy-seven thousand bullets were loaded aboard a freighter bound for Cyprus.

The cylinders arrived safely at the port of Famagusta and were driven to the home of Andreas Lambrou, the dentist, where a hideout had been prepared. Lambrou and his mother went to work to cut the guns free.

EOKA in Nicosia was still under the leadership of Polycarpos Georgadjis, who was living with his aides at the Gabrielides' home. After committing a number of street murders in October and November the groups had paused to prepare for the next round. Georgadjis moved about town conferring with section leaders. The regular champagne sessions with British officials continued in the Gabrielides' bar, but now Georgadjis and his two aides stayed locked in a bedroom; there was no fear of searches while the bar was tenanted by British "Security."

Georgadjis at this time controlled not only gunmen who shot down civilians; he also exercised powers of life and death over his own followers. Yannakis Stefanides, the young deputy leader, who had taken over after the collapse of the Nicosia organization in February 1957, had offended his superiors in several ways. He had failed to be on duty at the required times; he had taken trips about the island in defiance of orders restricting him to one area; he had been sent to Larnaca to lead groups there, and had returned without permission because he was not happy among strangers; and finally, he had broken EOKA's rigid code by indulging in a love affair and refusing to give up the girl. All this Georgadjis reported to Grivas; and when the offense was compounded by further disobedience, Grivas ordered him shot. He was executed under Georgadjis' supervision.

Grivas was alarmed at the drift toward compromise which, to him, meant a "sell-out" of the sacred principle of Enosis—union with Greece, for which he had fought for four years. In December the United Nations debate ended in yet another temporizing resolution calling for continued efforts to reach a "peaceful, democratic and just solution." The United States sided with Britain and swung the Latin American vote against an Indian resolution which attempted to stop the slide toward partition with a resolution recognizing the "integrity" of Cyprus. Makarios and Averoff persuaded Grivas to suspend activities during the debate, and when it was over urged him to maintain a cease-fire "for as long as possible" despite continuing British military operations. "All sides have tried to create an atmosphere of detente in the last few months, each for its own reasons,'' Makarios reported, and he had hopes that a solution might emerge from the confusion.[1]

A year before, the United States had openly favored independence as a solution; but now Washington had swung round again toward the Anglo-Turkish point of view, largely because of the alarming international picture.[2] The Russians were creating a fresh crisis over Berlin; the Iraqi monarch had been overthrown in July 1958; and Greece and Turkey were edging closer to an open clash over Cyprus at a time when NATO was trying to display a solid front toward Communist advances. There was no doubt as to which of the three member countries had least strategic significance to the NATO alliance and to the United States. As Averoff wrote to Grivas on December 27, 1958:

> On reading the delegates' speeches you would expect us to obtain a nine-tenths majority—yet we get nothing . . . what the delegates say in public is of no value; their votes are cast entirely on the basis of self-interest, and the British and Turkish influence far outweigh ours.[3]

However, Averoff observed, the great majority of delegates had deplored partition as a solution and vaunted the idea of independence, toward which both the Greek government and Makarios were now leaning. The Greek and Cypriot leaders feared that Britain, weary of the cost in men and money, was considering either forcible partition or a phased withdrawal which would eventually lead to a form of *de facto* partition as the warring communities withdrew into their own strongholds.

Premier Adnan Menderes' overspending on development programs had created grave financial problems in Turkey, and Ankara was ready to bend to the pressures of American and European creditors in return for further loans. In fact, the first step toward a compromise solution had already been taken at a meeting behind the scenes in the United Nations building in New York, when the British envoy, Sir Pierson Dixon, and the Turkish foreign minister Fatin Zorlu met with Averoff and privately agreed to work seriously for a solution.

Averoff and Zorlu met again at a NATO conference in Paris on December 18 and consolidated the agreement to negotiate through diplomatic channels. The Greek foreign minister and the Archbishop were having difficulty in persuading Grivas to maintain the cease-fire. British troops were continuing operations and harassing his groups, despite EOKA's suspension of action. And there were at that time two young

EOKA members awaiting execution in the Nicosia jail; Foot had refused reprieves and a bloody reprisal seemed certain. The men were to be hanged on December 19, a matter of hours after the meeting of Zorlu and Averoff in Paris. But as Sir Hugh Foot sat at Government House, awaiting the call that would tell him the executions had been performed, a message arrived from London. Premier Macmillan wished Sir Hugh to know that Zorlu had joined Averoff in asking that the hangings should not take place because of the destructive effect they would have on the current talks. Foot stopped the executions with twenty minutes to spare.

The growing indications of a "sell-out" by Athens persuaded Grivas that he must go to the center of affairs in Nicosia. Elaborate precautions would have to be taken. Antonis Georghiades was dispatched with messages for the Greek consul and for Deacon Anthimos, who must make provision for the presence of "Dighenis." Couriers reported that searches on the Limassol-Nicosia road had never been more rigorous. Cars were being stripped, hubcaps and seats removed. But the deacon had already prepared, with the help of Socrates Eliades, a new means of transporting fugitives between the towns—the tank trucks used in the past now being considered suspect. Behind the doors of a locked garage at his service station, Eliades had built a secret compartment between the cab of a truck and the back, converting the open vehicle into a closed van. The hideout was entered from beneath the van, which was filled with furniture and bric-a-brac. Eliades drove the vehicle to Limassol with Niki Anthimos, the deacon's wife, beside him in the cab.

Nicosia was reached without mishap, and Georghiades was welcomed to the Eliades home. He visited in the next few days, the consul, the bishop of Kitium, and others, and his reports on his meetings with these political figures calmed his chief's more extravagant fears. At last, on December 24, 1958, Grivas bowed to pressure from Athens and issued a proclamation temporarily suspending operations as a gesture of respect for the United Nations resolution. "We offer," he said, "an opportunity for a solution in an atmosphere of peace. What will the enemy do?" [4]

They would temporize. While the situation had so far improved as to permit a conciliatory meeting between Sir Hugh Foot and Makarios' deputy, Bishop Anthimos, military operations continued in the Troodos mountains, although the most strenuous curfews and searches were ended. Throughout January 1959, the British persisted with propaganda on behalf of the moribund "Macmillan Plan," and the governor felt it appropriate to warn, for a last time, that there could be no bargaining with violence.

The bargaining was in fact proceeding in Paris, where Zorlu and Averoff held a series of meetings between January 17 and 22. The basis of their discussions was an independent Cyprus with both Enosis and partition excluded; the British would be given their bases, and some Greek and Turkish military presence in the island was foreseen. In his letters to Makarios, Grivas expressed an almost frenzied suspicion: the consul and the bishop were not telling Georghiades the full truth; Averoff was tricking him over the supply of arms; they were all terrified that Grivas would form a political alliance of his own, to demand a voice at the peace talks; there was evidence that Averoff was even involved in a plot to betray him to the British police, so that he could be removed from the scene, while a Greco-Turkish agreement was forced upon the unwilling Cypriot people. The conciliatory words of Averoff, the apologies of the consul, and Makarios' reminders that he, and not Grivas, was the political leader of the struggle did little to soothe Grivas.

Georghiades returned to the Limassol hideout in mid-January to report in detail his conversations with the consul and the bishop of Kitium. It seemed to Grivas that they had again told his aide as little as possible; and when, on February 5, he heard the news that the Greek and Turkish premiers were meeting in Zurich to decide the island's fate, he decided to leave at once for the capital. Socrates Eliades and the deacon's wife drove down to Limassol once more to pick up Grivas and Georghiades near their hideout. Grivas disembarked safely in the dark, tree-shrouded yard behind Eliades' house, little the worse for the ninety minutes he spent packed into the truck's secret compartment with Georghiades.

But events had overtaken him. On February 10, 1959, it was announced that the premiers of Greece and Turkey, in the space of six days, had reached full agreement on Cyprus, and a conference would be convened in London to complete the work begun in Paris barely two months before. Archbishop Makarios, persuaded that the British and Turks would concede no more at this stage, added his signature to those of the British, Greek, and Turkish prime ministers on February 19, 1959. The foundation was laid for the creation of an independent sovereign state of Cyprus, ruled by a Greek-Cypriot president with a Turkish vice president who held the right of veto in foreign affairs. A house of representatives would be established in the proportion of seventy percent Greek to thirty percent Turkish members (although Turks formed only eighteen percent of the population). The civil service and police would be shared in the same way, and the main towns would have separate Greek and Turkish municipalities. A treaty of alliance established the presence of nine hundred and fifty Greek and six hundred and fifty Turkish troops on the island, token forces which, it was hoped, would help to guarantee the independence of Cyprus in some undefined fashion. As for the British bases, their shape, size and number would be worked out later by British and Cypriot representatives.

Three points in these agreements were especially offensive to Grivas, and indeed to the majority of Greek Cypriots: the presence of Turkish troops, the advent of separate municipalities, and a seventy–thirty ratio in the police and civil service. Makarios himself liked them little enough; but he was faced with insistent demands from Premier Karamanlis and from Averoff—not to mention the ultimatums of the British, who insisted that he sign on the afternoon of the last meeting of the premiers, because Mr. Macmillan was due to fly next day to Moscow.

The Archbishop felt certain that to reject the agreements would be to bring partition upon the island, in one form or another. The British ministers had given him until mid-morning of the following day to make his decision, and before that deadline arrived he telephoned his submission to the Foreign Office in London. It was, he said later, "the better of two bad things." [5]

The Archbishop was now free to return to Cyprus, and on March 1, 1959, he was received by wildly enthusiastic crowds. But of Grivas, who was to leave the island under the terms of the agreement, there was no sign. Nor did he send so much as a representative to welcome his partner in revolution. The agreements, Grivas complained, had been reached behind his back and several basic elements of them were still being withheld: how large, for example, were the British bases to be? How many troops would the British maintain on the island? In a letter to the Greek consul he observed that, from all he had heard, they would be able to take over every key point in the island at any time they wished. It was his view that the so-called agreements were no more than a "surrender"; and he would not acclaim them as a victory or a vindication of the struggle, whatever shameful flatteries or promises were made. [6]

The terms of a general amnesty for all prisoners and wanted men were negotiated by Foot and Makarios without consultation with Grivas, who made his demands clear in writing. These were simple enough: a complete and universal amnesty for every member of EOKA, in prison or out. Foot's attempts to release the men in stages, and to exile some of the most serious offenders (or greatest heroes, depending on the point of view) were to be rejected outright. As for his own departure, Grivas remarked that he would choose his time and mode of transport; nor need the Greek government trouble to supply him with an armed escort; he could provide his own.

After some hesitation, the governor capitulated and insisted on one condition: that certain "troublesome" EOKA leaders, who had been moved to jails in Britain some time previously, should stay out of Cyprus until the formal declaration of the Republic.

Not until March 9 did Grivas meet personally with Makarios. Certain "negative" phrases in the final cease-fire proclamation that Grivas had prepared were deleted at the Archbishop's request in case they should undermine public faith in the settlement. There were other meetings with Makarios over the next few days, and the breach was, however uneasily, smoothed over.

On March 13, in accordance with the terms of the agreement, EOKA handed in its weapons, or enough of them to satisfy protocol; they would, in any case, become the property of the new Republic in a few months' time. There was no more to be done: Grivas began a round of farewell visits. He acted as godfather to the latest addition to the family of Marios and Elli Christodoulides, who had sheltered him in Limassol for two and a half years. The child was christened Kikki, after Grivas' wife. Next there was a farewell party at the Gabrielides' home in Nicosia, where forty-seven district leaders and other EOKA men were gathered. When all were assembled, Grivas appeared in a doorway, dressed in a guerrilla suit that had been specially prepared for him by the women of EOKA—knitted jersey, breeches, bandolier, and beret; on his hip, a revolver. He made a long and emotional speech, then embraced each man and woman in turn even those he was meeting for the first time.

Next day, he was driven to a friend's house to meet a group of influential Cypriots who had helped EOKA in various ways, and a handful of local newspaper editors. The Archbishop and the Greek consul were present; and when the speeches were over, the party set out for the airport. First was the consul's car, carrying Grivas and Georghiades; then the Archbishop's; and last, other church dignitaries bringing up the rear. Since Grivas' departure had been kept secret on British insistence, the road was almost empty. A small group of police and intelligence officers had gathered at the airport for a glimpse of the man they had so long pursued. Ignoring them, Grivas said his last farewells and boarded a Dakota aircraft of the Royal Hellenic Air Force which waited to fly him to victory ceremonies in Athens. It had been four years and one hundred twenty-eight days since he had landed in Cyprus to begin the revolution.

The eighteen months that had elapsed between the signing of the London agreement and formal declaration of the new Cypriot Republic were occupied with details of the transfer of power. Intensive bargaining over the size of the British sovereign bases and the amount of financial aid Britain would give to Cyprus caused repeated delays; but eventually Makarios, having reduced the British demand for a base area of one hundred twenty square miles to ninety-nine, and raised the amount of aid from an unspecified sum to twelve and one-half million pounds, with a pledge of more to come, pronounced himself satisfied. Sir Hugh Foot, last British governor of Cyprus, made a ceremonial departure from the island in August 1960, aboard a Royal Navy destroyer.

Makarios Becomes President

Independence of the Republic of Cyprus was declared on August 16, 1960, but it satisfied neither Greek Cypriot *Enosists* nor the Turks who sought partition. From the outset rivalries and hatreds both inside the two factions and between them made the creation of a viable government problematic. It may be said that the Republic's most remarkable achievement to date has been its survival.

Archbishop Makarios was elected president with sixty-seven percent of the popular vote, and the British administrators departed in friendly style, leaving behind several thousand troops in the "sovereign bases." Elections to the House of Representatives were held, the Greeks being alloted sixty-five seats, the Turks fifteen. Dr. Fazil Kuchuk, as vice president, had extensive powers of veto. Makarios' cabinet was a judicious mixture of EOKA personalities and the best Greek-Cypriot brains. Glafkos Clerides, the British-trained lawyer (who had dispatched Sir Hugh Foot's message to Grivas, warning him against his campaign of sabotage in 1958), became speaker of the house and deputy-president of the Republic. Polycarpos Georgadjis, the EOKA chieftain, was named minister of the interior. Other EOKA leaders returned to civilian life. Nicos Sampson, the gunman, was given amnesty and released by the British. He launched a newspaper, *Combat,* and spurred its circulation with accounts of assassinations performed by his "execution squads." In 1970, he was elected to the House.

The Republic prospered with the help of Western aid and the income from the bases, its gross national product rising steadily over the years. New roads and hotels were built, new industries created. Now that the island was a part of the British Commonwealth, Queen Elizabeth II paid it a visit and was introduced to the Archbishop.

It was not long, however, before Makarios' authority was seriously challenged by Grivas who, on his return to Greece, had been decorated, promoted to general and retired on full pay. Enosis, the cause for which he had fought, remained a dream, and Grivas—charging that vital clauses in the London agreement had been withheld from him— repudiated the settlement and accused the Greek government of betraying the Cypriots. The foreign minister, Averoff, replied that the administration, "having honoured Mr. Grivas to an exaggerated degree" would now regard him as any other politician.

In Cyprus, EOKA split into warring factions, the larger behind Makarios, the small, uncompromising Enosist group for "the Leader." In accordance with the terms of the agreement, EOKA was to hand in all its arms, but the Grivas faction kept back their best, including the one hundred new automatics smuggled in shortly before the final truce, thus forming a base for the first of the "private armies" which were to harry Cyprus over the next decade.

The Turks, already dissatisfied with the way the London agreement was being implemented, were provoked by Grivas' new call for Enosis and began to smuggle in their own arms from abroad. The conflict that arose over Turkish-Cypriot claims to thirty percent of all official posts was to remain the main stumbling block to a permanent settlement. Not that there was much else on which the two sides could agree: in foreign policy, for instance, the Turks abhorred Makarios' overtures to the nonaligned Afro-Asian nations; and the Turkish Cypriots as a community felt that they were deprived of many things that the Greeks could take for granted. Water, power, and other facilities were inadequate, housing often squalid, educational standards lagged; and racial memories of centuries of Turkish mastery were never far beneath the surface. Feelings ran high over the Republic's token army and its divided municipal councils—one Greek, one Turkish in every town. No less than forty percent of the army envisaged by the agreement was to be Turkish, and Kuchuk insisted that these units function independently of the Greeks; Makarios wanted an integrated force. He also attempted to unify the municipal councils or bring them under control of the central government, only to be met with fierce opposition from the Turks, who stopped paying rates and taxes when the Greeks threatened a unilateral alteration of the constitution. Violent incidents began to recur.

The crisis deepened as traumatic developments occurred abroad. The government of Adnan Menderes and Fatin Zorlu had been brought down by a military coup, and both men were convicted of treason and publicly hanged. In Athens, Premier Karamanlis had resigned at the climax of a dispute with the Greek royal family. Both countries were thus virtually leaderless, when, on December 5, 1963, President Makarios informed the British, Greek, and Turkish governments that he intended to abolish the seventy–thirty ethnic ratio in the civil service and unify the town councils. Ankara quickly rejected this unilateral revision of the constitution. Shortly before Christmas 1963, civil war returned to Cyprus.

The precise incident which sparked the conflagration is of little significance; both sides were spoiling for a fight. The Turks had been for months secretly training men. The Greeks, besides controlling the police, had their own clandestine army, trained by EOKA veterans and divided into companies with scouts, radio operators, and medical teams. They were thus stronger and better organized than were their opponents.

A shooting war began on Christmas Eve, when Greek units launched an attack on a predominantly Turkish suburb of the capital to rescue a pocket of surrounded Greeks. Turkish gunposts were overwhelmed, women and children killed, and hundreds of hostages were taken by both sides while appeals went to Ankara. As a warning, Turkey sent jet fighters low over Nicosia, and rumors spread that an invasion fleet had set out across the forty miles of sea from the Turkish mainland. Athens threatened that if the Turks intervened, Greek forces would do likewise. The NATO council issued calls for peace, but only after several hundred people had been killed did the warring parties agree to be kept apart by a British peace force. A truce committee under British chairmanship drew up an agreement on neutral zones, and hostages were returned between the two sides.

Attention now focused on the creation of an international peace-keeping force for the island while negotiations proceeded. The British sought American backing for the dispatch of a force drawn from NATO armies, but Makarios was determined on resort to the United Nations—NATO being, in his eyes, a body too deeply involved in cold war politics. The efforts of George Ball, President Johnson's envoy, who spent three days in February 1964 urging upon Makarios the NATO idea, were without success, and demonstrations against the Anglo-American peace plan were held in Cyprus before the office of the British high commissioner and the U.S. embassy—which was later damaged by bombs. As some six hundred American dependents left for the safety of Beirut, Makarios apologized to Ambassador Fraser Wilkins for "a revolting crime by abominable men who wanted to destroy friendship between the U.S. and Cyprus.''

The problem now went before the United Nations, and on March 3, 1964, a resolution was passed authorizing a U.N. peace force for Cyprus. Before it could be mustered, fighting again broke out, bringing fresh threats from Ankara. Greece's newly elected premier, George Papandreou, leader of a Center-Left coalition, promised military support for the Greek Cypriots. Greek officers were hurriedly recalled from NATO headquarters in Izmir, while Greek warships cruised off Rhodes, ready to intercept a Turkish force said to be embarking for Cyprus. It is doubtful whether Turkey at this time possessed either the resolution or the competence to conduct a large-scale invasion by sea; but at all events, thanks to determined action by President Johnson, none came. The Turkish premier, Ismet Inonu, said later [1]

> The invasion of Cyprus was fixed for June 4, 1964, but one day before, I was warned by Washington not to use American arms for purposes not approved by America. Mr. Johnson said that if the Russians took action, our NATO guarantees might not hold. We might also face the danger of impeachment at the United Nations. In half an hour, we would be left without an ally.

Before the end of March, the main body of the U.N. peace force, which would eventually total some seven thousand troops from Canada, Sweden, Ireland, Denmark, and Finland, had landed in Cyprus, under the command of an Indian general; they were followed by a Finnish diplomat, Sakari Tuomioja, who was to act as U.N. mediator. On March 27, 1964, U.N. forces, known as UNFICYP, officially assumed the task of preserving the peace.

Greece was five hundred miles away, and it had been proved during the Kokkina fighting that the Greek Air Force could give the Cypriots no support. Andreas Papandreou, Greece's minister of state at the time, explained:

> . . . it was technically impossible. Cyprus was far from Greek air bases and our fighters would have had no more than two minutes flying time over Cyprus. We would therefore only have provoked Turkey into further action, without offering substantive aid to the Cypriot ground forces.[1]

For eighteen months, Cyprus was quiet—or nearly so. The most stubborn problem continued to be the refractory Grivas, who caused minor clashes by sending his patrols too close to Turkish positions, by erecting new fortifications and otherwise upsetting the Turks in their sandbagged enclaves. But however eager all concerned might be to curb Grivas, it seemed that only an order from Athens could dislodge him; and the government there, faced with a challenge nearer home, was slow to act.

— 26 —

Cyprus and the Junta

On April 21, 1967, a group of unknown army officers conducted a military coup in Athens, seizing control of the government and placing George Papandreou, leader of the Center-Left opposition, under house arrest. This military junta used rumors of a Papandreou-Communist conspiracy as a pretext to take over Greece on the eve of national elections which the coalition led by Papandreou was generally expected to win.

The new regime soon found itself under pressure from the United States and its allies in NATO to promote a rapid settlement of the Cyprus problem through direct talks with leaders of the Turkish government. Accordingly, George Papadopolous, leader of the junta, sought to settle the conflict with Prime Minister Demirel of Turkey at a summit meeting held on September 9, 1967. Dean Acheson's proposal for union of Cyprus with Greece together with the establishment of Turkish military bases in the island formed the basis for their discussions. Makarios had rejected this idea as tantamount to partition when it was first put forward in 1964; but Papadopolous was hopeful that if an accord could be reached with Turkey, the Cypriot president might be persuaded to go along with it. Demirel, however, insisted on the validity of the London agreement of 1959 which specifically barred Enosis, and also required the withdrawal of all Greek military forces on the island before any other matter was discussed. When the talks collapsed the Greek Cypriots were by no means displeased, for union with a Greece dominated by the authoritarian junta had small appeal to most of them.

Any remaining hopes of reaching an accommodation with Ankara were destroyed by Grivas in November 1967, when he initiated a violent attack to drive Turkish Cypriots from positions commanding the

Nicosia-Limassol road, one of the island's main arteries. Houses in the villages of Ayios Theodoros and Kophinou were demolished by artillery and twenty-seven Turkish Cypriots were killed. Turkish jets screamed low over Cyprus while Turkish troops were reported to be boarding an invasion fleet. Ankara now openly demanded that the Greek government recall Grivas to Athens and withdraw all Greek troops stationed in Cyprus since 1964.

The junta yielded to the Turkish terms with surprising speed. The two villages occupied by Grivas were evacuated on orders from Athens and Grivas himself was recalled to Greece on November 29. After President Johnson's emissary, Cyrus Vance, had arrived in the area to talk with Greek and Turkish leaders, it was agreed that all non-Cypriot forces beyond the small token number authorized by the London agreement should be withdrawn.

Ankara's diplomatic triumph was now complete. Turkey had forced Grivas and several thousand Greek troops out of Cyprus. Feelings on the island ran high against what was considered a surrender by the junta to the Turks. Makarios, who had consistently opposed talks based on a NATO-sponsored solution, emerged from the debacle in a strengthened position; and in the presidential elections of 1968 Greek Cypriots returned him by an overwhelming majority for a second five-year term. Makarios' rival, Dr. Takis Evdokas, leader of the extreme right National party, which served as a political front for Grivas, obtained less than five percent of the vote.

But Makarios now found himself embroiled in a bitter conflict with the junta in Athens and the admirers of Grivas in Cyprus, many of whom believed that the Archbishop, in signing the 1959 London agreement, had betrayed the sacred cause of Enosis.

Makarios' policies were in many ways at odds with those of the junta. He was a neutralist who wished to remain on friendly terms with Communist governments and Arab states that looked to Moscow for support, aid, and arms, while the junta was a military dictatorship which displayed unquestioning loyalty toward the United States, NATO, and "the defense of Western civilisation" against a Communist threat. There was, too, the possibility that Makarios, who had been on reasonably good terms with George Papandreou, might allow Cyprus to be used as a base for a resistance movement against the junta. The new regime did not trust him, and Papadopolous fiercely resented Makarios' opposition to his plans to settle the problem with Turkey once and for all by bringing Cyprus into the NATO sphere.

The junta's fears might seem inadequate reasons for an attempt to remove Makarios by assassination, but there was no doubt in his mind that its agents were behind such an attempt in February 1970. The presidential helicopter was machine-gunned as it took off in Nicosia, but the pilot, seriously wounded, was able to land safely. The Archbishop, though shaken, survived unscathed. The Cyprus police satisfied themselves that officers from Greece had engineered the plot, but their evidence was insufficient to win a conviction. Makarios, however, stated bluntly in an interview that the junta wanted him removed from the scene so that they might "make us share the island as they like with Turkey." [1]

The junta—having purged Cyprus of the Greek "military liberals" placed there during the Papandreou regime—now began to send over its own hand-picked officers and created a network of agents who would try to ensure that the influence of Athens was felt in the proper places.

Greek versus Greek

The deterioration in relations with Athens came to a head with an open confrontation in mid-1971 when Archbishop Makarios paid a week-long visit to Moscow, returning with pledges of support from the Soviet leaders for Cypriot independence. An emissary from Premier Papadopolous was dispatched to Nicosia with an ultimatum for "double Enosis" or the resignation of Makarios as president. Makarios replied on July 12, 1971, publicly rejecting pressure on him to step down.

In an attempt to break this deadlock, Grivas, who had been watching events from Athens since his removal from command of all Cypriot forces in 1968, returned by fishing boat in September 1971. Now seventy-four, but still alert, he set about organizing a new irredentist force commited to Enosis. In leaflets claiming the backing of the motherland and calling on the "glorious fighters of EOKA" to arise again, he announced a new struggle, to be led once more by "Dighenis." That the junta intended to use Grivas as a lever against Makarios seems unquestionable: they officially informed the Cypriot president on the eve of his arrival in Athens for peace talks that Grivas had "vanished" from the Greek capital and might be in Cyprus.

A series of arms raids on police stations began in November 1971, but for several months, Grivas' presence was felt chiefly as a shadow portending more serious trouble. He remained in hiding and ignored Makarios' suggestion that he become the island's defense minister.

The arrival of a large consignment of arms, ordered from Czechoslovakia by the Cyprus government, brought about a further confrontation with the junta. Makarios had no intention of allowing the three hundred tons of weapons and explosives either to reach the National Guard, where the junta's chosen officers might dispose of them as they pleased or to be seized by Grivas. A quantity of the Czech material was therefore transported to his palace in Nicosia where its discovery a few days later caused an international furor. The junta accused Makarios of plotting against Athens, while Turkey—apparently fearing a conflict between Greek and Greek which might be used as a pretext for an attack on Turkish Cypriots, or a takeover by the junta—moved troops to the coast and prepared an air drop. Simultaneously, the island's three leading bishops made the belated discovery that it was uncanonical for the head of the Church to be also head of state and called on Makarios to resign, a move which the Archbishop denounced as junta-inspired.

By agreeing to yield the Czech arms to UNFICYP, while offering to abdicate if such was the Cypriot people's desire, Makarios caused a massive demonstration of popular support. Crowds beneath the presidential windows, shouting their protests against "the Judas bishops" and the junta, called on the president to remain. Makarios thus emerged triumphant from another crisis, and the junta, bowing to the wishes of Turkey, publicly reaffirmed Greece's faith in the 1960 treaty which outlawed Enosis. With this volte-face, the junta abandoned, at least for the time being, its attempt to impose a solution on Cyprus.

But if the junta had accepted, however temporarily, the status quo, Grivas could never relax his demand for Enosis. He turned now to a revived guerrilla campaign of sabotage, robbing, and dynamiting police stations and shooting an occasional informer, according to the old EOKA formula; the island's life, however, continued almost unchanged, since Cypriots had long been hardened to such events.

The unopposed entry of Makarios on his third term as president in February 1973 reflected the hold he retained on the Greek Cypriot people. The Grivas supporters' "National Democratic Party," which in 1968 had won such a minute percentage of the vote, avoided further humiliation by not contesting the election.

Grivas continued his campaign against Makarios and his policies, using most of the same tactics that had been successful in his struggle with the British. But new factors whose existence Grivas was reluctant to admit tended to swing the balance, this time, against him. First, he faced as an opponent not a British governor at the head of an alien occupation army but a leader, in Makarios, whose popularity was demonstrably higher than his own. Second, his much diminished following had ranged against it both the mass of public opinion and a strong paramilitary police force under an indigenous leadership that had been tempered in years of guerrilla warfare and was attuned to Grivas' tactics. He had forfeited much of the respect and awe commanded by the legendary 'Dighenis' who rallied patriotic Cypriots against foreign domination. Grivas died of a heart attack in January, 1974, at the age of 75, while still in hiding and with his dream of Enosis still unfulfilled.

Epilogue

At Grivas' funeral there were emotional scenes as the old warrior's most devout followers pledged themselves to continue the struggle for union with Greece. Nicos Sampson, the former gunman, draped himself in a Greek flag and delivered a speech promising that the "pure flame of enosis" would be kept alive as "The Leader" would have wished; and indeed Sampson was destined to inherit Grivas' mantle for a brief and inglorious spell.

To most Cypriots, it had become clear that each renewal of violence, so far from bringing Enosis closer, shifted it further from the realm of possibility; but Grivas' followers, calling themselves now "EOKA B", and no longer controlled by the old general's experienced hand, began to demonstrate an increasingly lethal vigor; President Makarios' 3,000 man "tactical reserve" responded in kind with counter-terror tactics. The military junta in Athens, now led by Brigadier Demetrios Ioannides, latest in a series of strongmen, controlled and supplied EOKA B through its hand-picked body of officers at the head of the 10,000 strong Cyprus National Guard, which they were officially supposed to be training. Ioannides had himself served as a Greek officer on Cyprus in the sixties, an experience that had confirmed his distaste for the neutralism of Makarios. This inflexible personality controlled ESA, the Greek military police, a force that he had used to topple Col. George Papadopolous from the presidency on November 25, 1973; very soon Ioannides, a hard-bitten anti-communist, was planning a second coup, this time in Cyprus.

When Makarios received documentary evidence from his agents that the junta's new leaders were preparing, through the National Guard and its allies in EOKA B, to escalate the clandestine war against his regime, he answered the challenge with an open letter which charged that EOKA B and the Greek officers in Cyprus had as their aims his own assassination and the liquidation of the Cyprus Republic. The junta, Makarios wrote, was behind the criminal activity of recent months, and it was responsible for past attempts on his life; yet he had always tried to cooperate with Athens in the national interest, and even now did not wish to end that cooperation. He was not, however, as he suggested, a district governor appointed by the junta, but an elected leader of a great section of the Greek world, and as such he demanded appropriate treatment. As a first step, Makarios demanded the recall to Athens of the Greek officers he charged with plotting against his life; then he would reform the National Guard.

On July 15, 1974, two weeks after the dispatch of this letter, several of its predictions were fulfilled: in a military coup engineered by the officers from Athens, parliamentary rule was overthrown and Makarios himself barely escaped with his life. As shells fired by the National Guard guns and tanks reduced the Presidential Palace to a burning shambles, and his personal security force was overwhelmed by superior odds, Makarios fled through a rear entrance to the palace grounds and along a dry river bed to a road. Then, in a car borrowed from a passerby, he was driven across the mountains to the little port of Paphos, where he broadcast news of his escape, and rallied resistance.

The leaders of the coup were at the same time announcing over the captured CBC radio station Makarios' death in the fighting. As the new "president", they installed Nicos Sampson, the former gunman, who, in 1957, had been sentenced to death by the British, amnestied at the end of the rebellion, and now headed a modest publishing house of which the mainstay was a daily newspaper *Makhi* (Combat). As leader of the small "Progressive Party", a small splinter party in the House of Representatives, Sampson had recently turned against Makarios, assailing him as the "Pope-Caesar of Cyprus." An unhappier presidential choice than Sampson would be difficult to conceive. He had neither the temperament nor the ability for any such task and was, besides, the Greek most execrated by the Turkish Cypriots, against whom he had led several bloody onslaughts in the communal fighting of 1963.

Makarios' supporters resisted gallantly, but they could not long hold out against the well-planned assault of the National Guard, which had used its heavy armor to seize key positions. Makarios, finding himself trapped by land and sea in Paphos, arranged with officers of UNFICYP to be taken by RAF helicopter to nearby British base. From there, on July 16, he was flown via Malta to London and on to New York, to lead a protest at the United Nations Security Council meeting.

But it was too late, now, for words: Turkey, alarmed and angered at what they considered the Greek seizure of the island, had mounted a police action of its own to counter the coup. On July 20, 1974, after rejecting pleas from the United States, Great Britain, NATO, and the U.N., Premier Bulent Ecevit gave the order to invade, and waves of Turkish troops and armor crossed the 40-mile strait separating the two countries to land at dawn along Cyprus's northern coast. Turkish jets bombed and strafed Nicosia, and an airdrop of paratroopers farther inland linked up with the main invasion force to form a salient pointed at the capital. Soon, some 40,000 Turkish troops were in control of a broad swath of the island stretching from Kyrenia on the north coast to Nicosia. Fighting was heavy: there were thousands of casualties, and more than 200,000 people were left homeless as the Turkish advance pushed on in defiance of a unanimous U.N. Security Council call for a cease-fire.

Turkey's military superiority, and the 600 miles of sea between Athens and Cyprus, which allowed Greek fighter bombers only a few moments over the island before they must return for refueling, made a counterinvasion impossible. Greece was confronted with political, diplomatic, and military humiliation. In Athens, even the semblance of government was crumbling. Civilian ministers and fellow officers alike deserted Brigadier Ioannides, and came together to force his resignation. On July 23, 1974, three days after the Turkish landings, a triumvirate of senior Greek generals announced that government would be restored to civilian hands, and former Premier Constantine Karamanlis, who had lived in self-imposed exile in Paris since 1963, following his resignation after a conflict with the Greek royal family, was recalled once more to take up the reins of power. Karamanlis, a moderate conservative who had led the country from 1956 to 1962 (and who had joined with Britain and Turkey in the 1960 agreement guaranteeing the independence of Cyprus), quickly restored basic civil liberties, freed political prisoners, and set about the task of repairing the damage done by seven years of military rule.

With the junta toppled, Nicos Sampson was removed from power in Cyprus as brusquely as he had been pushed into it; he was replaced by Glafkos Clerides, the British-trained lawyer and wartime RAF flyer who had served as Makarios' deputy since the first days of the Republic. He was welcomed by all sides, with the exception of the discredited EOKA *B* extremists. As Interim President, there was no one the Turks would find it easier to get along with. One of his first actions was to hold a conciliatory meeting with Rauf Denktash, his Turkish-Cypriot counterpart, with whom he had spent countless hours between 1963 and 1974 trying to negotiate a communal settlement. But there was little that Clerides could do now in face of the overwhelming Turkish military presence in the island.

The Turkish army, defying the cease-fire and ignoring a hastily convened peace conference in Geneva pushed on, looting many Greek homes in its advance. Interracial conflict was revived, with tragic consequences on both sides. The peace talks that had begun in July broke down in August, and the Turks drove a wedge across the island to seize the port of Famagusta and take control of the entire northern third of Cyprus, including most of the area that attracted the island's lucrative tourist trade. In protest, Karamanlis withdrew Greek forces from NATO and massed troops along the Turkish-Greek border; but he was powerless to assist Greek Cypriots in their hour of need.

With Cyprus effectively partitioned, and no outside aid forthcoming, there was much talk among Greeks of a new guerrilla war to drive out the intruders; there was no shortage of potential fighters. But even the most optimistic knew that they would find the going hard. Greek irregulars would have to take the initiative in barren, flat terrain behind the lines of an occupation force that had already proved its aptitude for swift and bloody reprisals.

On the international front, U.N. resolutions were ignored, and little effort was made by Britain, a co-guarantor of the 1960 agreement, the United States, or Soviet Russia to put pressure on Ankara to withdraw the Turkish troops. Many Greeks even accused the United States of organizing the crisis for its own ends, pointing out that Secretary of State Kissinger refused to recognize Archbishop Makarios as president on his arrival in New York as an exile, and had rebuffed demands in the Senate that arms for Turkey should be suspended until its forces in Cyprus withdrew to the agreed truce line. In the face of a *fait accompli*, Dr. Kissinger apparently saw little reason to anger Ankara—regarded as a more useful ally than Athens—at a time when U.S. officials expected that Greece's withdrawal from NATO, which left a wide gap in the alliance, would be neither complete nor longlasting. A key to this view was seen in the admission of George Mavros, Greece's new foreign minister, who said, "We are condemned to friendship with our Turkish neighbours."

No peaceful resolution of the conflict that met the wishes of the Greek Cypriot majority could be conceived by any of those concerned with it. Yet if the tragedy of Cyprus has one clear message, it is that any solution imposed from outside on these devoted and stubborn islanders cannnot endure.

Makhairas, the twelfth century chronicler of Cyprus, wrote that "the poor Cypriots are a much-enduring people, and God in his Mercy avenges them; they make no sign at all." That passivity, nursed through ages of foreign domination, vanished in the turmoil of the years between 1954 and 1974; and although the scale of the conflict, as of the island itself, was relatively small, the issues confronted were universal, and the lessons to be learned are of import to a wider world.

Notes

Introduction

1. The records of Cyprus begin with the Pharaoh Thothmes III and the Egyptian occupation of the island in the fifteenth century B.C. In the Old Testament, it appears as Kittim, named after a great-grandson of Noah.
2. Moneypenny and Buckle, *Life of Disraeli,* Vol. II, p. 1163.
3. Luke, *Cyprus,* p. 180.
4. Storrs, *Orientations,* p. 473.
5. Grivas, *Guerrilla Warfare and EOKA's Struggle,* p. 1.
6. Ethnikos Laikos Apeleftherotikos Stratos (National Popular Liberation Front).
7. Grivas, *Memoirs,* p. 10.
8. Archbishop Makarios, in an interview with the authors, Nicosia, July 1962.
9. *Ibid.*
10. *Ibid.*
11. *Ibid.*
12. Eden, *Full Circle,* pp. 429, 446.

Chapter 1: Rumblings of Revolution

1. Estimated population January 1, 1956.
2. Grivas, *Memoirs,* p. 17.
3. In an interview with the authors, Nicosia, July 1962.
4. Athens Radio, July 25, 1952.
5. Grivas, *Memoirs,* p. 204.
6. Grivas, *Guerrilla Warfare,* p. 12.
7. Stephens, *A Place of Arms,* p. 135.

Chapter 2: Grivas Lands in Cyprus

1. *Terrorism in Cyprus: The Captured Documents*, p. 2.
2. Grivas, *Memoirs*, p. 25.
3. *The Captured Documents*, p. 3.

Chapter 3: Capture of the St. George

1. *Cyprus Mail*, January 1, 1955.
2. Annual pay for a constable was $750. The force was not even equipped with torches, the item having been struck from the budget.
3. "I thought that for one thing we could have a single anniversary celebration, instead of two, if we started on March 25." Makarios, in an interview with the authors, Nicosia, July 1962.
4. *The Captured Documents*, p. 5.
5. *Ibid.*
6. *Ibid.*
7. *Ibid.*, p. 11.

Chapter 4: The Revolt Begins

1. *Ibid.*, p. 42.
2. *Ibid.*, p. 12.
3. *Ibid.*, p. 17.
4. Until his assassination in 1970.
5. *Ibid.*, p. 20.
6. The diaries buried at Lyssi were discovered by British Intelligence during the summer of 1956, along with other documents and photographs, following betrayal by an EOKA member.
7. *Ibid.*, p. 23.
8. Grivas, *Memoirs*, p. 51.
9. *The Captured Documents*, p. 21.
10. Yanakis Droushiotis, in an interview with the authors, Nicosia, June 1963.
11. *Cyprus Mail*, April 3, 1955.
12. *The Captured Documents*, p. 23.
13. *Ibid.*, p. 46.
14. *Ibid.*, p. 25.

Chapter 5: Riots, Bombings, and Attacks

1. *The Captured Documents*, pp. 50–52.
2. *Ibid.*, p. 32. At this meeting Makarios also told Grivas to inform his agents in Athens that "arms could now be sent in consular bags to Cyprus. *The Church and Terrorism in Cyprus*, p. 29.

3. *The Captured Documents,* p. 60.
4. *Ibid.,* p. 61.

Chapter 6: Collision with Britain

1. Eden, *Full Circle,* p. 396.
2. The equivalent of a year's wages for the average young Cypriot.
3. Grivas, *Memoirs,* p. 39.
4. *Ibid.,* p. 40.
5. *Times of Cyprus,* February 10, 1956.
6. *Ibid.,* September 29, 1955.
7. *Ibid.,* September 4, 1955.
8. Interview with the authors, June 1962.
9. Grivas, *Memoirs,* p. 41.
10. Great Britain, *Parliamentary Papers* (Commons), "Tripartite Conference on Cyprus," Cmd. 9594, pp. 28–37.
11. Eden, *Full Circle,* p. 403.

Chapter 7: Harding Takes Charge

1. Grivas, *Memoirs,* p. 45.
2. Grivas, *Guerrilla Warfare,* p. 39.
3. *Ibid.*

Chapter 8: The Mountain Guerrillas

1. *Cyprus Mail,* November 27, 1955.

Chapter 9: Desperate Tactics

1. Grivas, *Memoirs,* p. 120.
2. *Times of Cyprus,* February 10, 1956.

Chapter 10: Makarios Is Exiled

1. For further details of EOKA's do-it-yourself arsenal see: Grivas, *Guerrilla Warfare* (Appendix VI: Explosives Made in Cyprus).
2. Athens Radio, quoted in *Times of Cyprus,* February 11, 1956.
3. Grivas, *Memoirs,* p. 126.
4. Eden, *Full Circle,* p. 403.
5. In an interview with the authors, Nicosia, June 1962.
6. *Ibid.*
7. *Ibid.*
8. *Ibid.*

Chapter 11: Grivas Takes Command

1. *Cyprus: EOKA's Campaign of Terror.* London: Central Office of Information, 1956.
2. EOKA leaflet, April 12, 1956. Public Information Office, Nicosia, Cyprus.
3. *Ibid.,* May 12, 1956.

Chapter 12: The Hunt for Grivas

1. *The Captured Documents,* p. 38.
2. Speech at Norwich, June 1, 1956. See *Cyprus: Background to Enosis.*
3. *The Captured Documents,* p. 38.
4. *Ibid.*
5. Grivas, *Guerrilla Warfare,* p. 43.

Chapter 13: Grivas Goes Underground

1. Grivas, *Memoirs,* p. 83.
2. *Ibid.,* p. 72.
3. *Times of Cyprus,* August 16, 1956.
4. Grivas, *Memoirs,* p. 87.
5. *Ibid.,* p. 87.

Chapter 14: No Surrender

1. The London *Daily Telegraph* of August 20, 1956, called the truce offer "tantamount to surrender" and "a desperate bid for breathing space." The *Times* of the same date drew an analogy with the situation in Kenya, when the Mau-Mau, bereft of the leadership of Jomo Kenyatta, began to feel the pressure of British security forces (once again led by Harding) and put out feelers to the government, which signified that "the gangs were beginning to crack."
2. Grivas, *Memoirs,* p. 89.
3. *Ibid.,* p. 90.
4. Grivas, *Guerrilla Warfare,* p. 66.
5. *Ibid.,* p. 68.

Chapter 15: Black November

1. Grivas, *Memoirs,* p. 99.
2. The last prosecution brought against a member of the security forces was on July 7, 1956. A British assistant superintendent was found guilty of assaulting three Cypriots brought in for interrogation. One had been beaten until he fell unconscious. A doctor said he had been examining civil assault cases for years without coming across such severe injuries. The defendant

had nothing to say, and was fined twenty-five pounds. *Times of Cyprus,* July 8, 1956.

Chapter 17: Debacle in the Mountains

1. *Times of Cyprus,* January 25, 1957.
2. Grivas, *Memoirs,* p. 110.
3. *Ibid.,* p. 112.
4. Grivas, *Guerrilla Warfare,* p. 52.
5. *Times of Cyprus,* March 11, 1957.
6. *The Guardian,* London, February 15, 1957.

Chapter 18: The Road to Independence

1. *Times of Cyprus,* May 26, 1957.
2. Grivas, *Memoirs,* p. 122.

Chapter 19: Breaking the Blockade

1. Foot, *A Start in Freedom,* p. 164.
2. Grivas, *Memoirs,* p. 136.

Chapter 20: Split Between Grivas and Makarios

1. Foot, *A Start in Freedom,* p. 154.
2. Grivas, *Memoirs,* p. 346.
3. *Ibid.,* p. 349.
4. *Ibid.,* p. 352.
5. *Ibid.,* p. 134.
6. *Ibid.,* p. 147.

Chapter 21: Civil War

1. Macmillan, *Riding the Storm,* pp. 669–671.
2. Foot, *A Start in Freedom,* p. 169.
3. *Ibid.,* p. 174.
4. Macmillan, *Riding the Storm,* p. 672.

Chapter 22: Counter-terror

1. Foot, *A Start in Freedom,* p. 175.
2. From the report of the coroner's inquest.
3. EOKA leaflet, October 7, 1958.
4. Grivas, *Memoirs,* p. 169.
5. *The Observer,* London, November 24, 1958.

Chapter 23: The Peace Conference

1. Grivas, *Memoirs,* p. 182.
2. Macmillan, *Riding the Storm,* p. 689.
3. Grivas, *Memoirs,* p. 182.
4. *Ibid.,* p. 184.
5. Stephens, *Cyprus: A Place of Arms,* p. 166.
6. Grivas, *Memoirs,* p. 192.

Chapter 24: Makarios Becomes President

1. Interview with the authors, June 12, 1964.

Chapter 25: Attempts toward Conciliation

1. Papandreou, *Democracy at Gunpoint,* p. 136.

Chapter 26: Greek versus Greek

1. *The Observer,* October 29, 1972.

Bibliography

The British colonial administration, on its departure from Cyprus in 1960, left in the archives of the new Republican government a considerable quantity of unpublished material—police files, official reports, and verbatim transcripts of court proceedings—relating to the years of revolution 1954–1959. Through the courtesy of President Makarios and the Ministry of the Interior, the authors were given access to this material. They examined copies of some 800 EOKA leaflets, orders, and letters in translation; police files on some 200 incidents of violence; transcripts of trials of EOKA members; and statistical records of deaths, injuries, and acts of violence. These documents were an invaluable aid in cross-checking the testimony of the EOKA witnesses on which this book is principally based. In the list of persons interviewed which follows, the names of some officials who were seen in the years prior to beginning work on this project have been included, when material from those interviews proved helpful. Affiliations of interviewees are as of the time of the authors' interview with them. The names of certain EOKA members have been omitted from the list since these men, although responsible for the deaths of others, were never formally accused or brought to trial, and some animus against them may persist in England or Cyprus.

Persons Interviewed

Averof, Evangelos, Foreign Minister of Greece, Athens, Greece.

Azinas, Andreas, Minister of Agriculture, Cyprus Government, Nicosia, Cyprus.

Belcher, Toby, United States Ambassador to Cyprus, Nicosia, Cyprus.

Castle, Barbara, Member of Parliament (Labour), London, England. (Later Britain's Minister of Labour.)

Chartas, Andreas. EOKA group commander, Nicosia district, Nicosia, Cyprus.

Christodoulides, Costas, EOKA group commander, Famagusta district, Famagusta, Cyprus.

185

Clerides, Glafkos, Speaker of the House of Representatives, Cyprus Government, Nicosia, Cyprus.

Driberg, Tom, Member of Parliament, Chairman of the British Labour Party, London, England.

Droushiotis, Yannis, EOKA group commander, Paphos district, Paphos, Cyprus.

Eliades, Socrates, merchant and import agent, Nicosia, Cyprus.

Foot, Sir Hugh, Governor of Cyprus. (later Lord Caradon), Nicosia, Cyprus.

Gabrielides, Gabriel, merchant and import agent, Nicosia, Cyprus.

Georgadjis, Polycarpos, Minister of the Interior, Cyprus Government, Nicosia, Cyprus.

Grivas, General George, leader of EOKA, Commander-in-Chief, Cyprus National Guard. Nicosia, Cyprus.

Grivas, Dr. Michael, physician, Nicosia, Cyprus.

Harding, Field-Marshal Sir John, Governor of Cyprus, Nicosia, Cyprus.

HjiMiltis, Demos, EOKA group commander, Limassol district, Limassol, Cyprus.

Inonu, Ismet, Prime Minister of Turkey, Ankara, Turkey.

Kafkallides, Lambros, personal aide to General Grivas, Nicosia, Cyprus.

Kendrew, Major-General Sir Douglas, Director of Operations, 1957–1958, Nicosia, Cyprus.

Kuchuk, Dr. Fazil, Vice-President of Cyprus. Nicosia, Cyprus.

Kokkinou, Loulla, chief of EOKA's communications network, Nicosia, Cyprus.

Koshis, Nicos, deputy EOKA group commander, Nicosia district, Nicosia, Cyprus.

Lagoudontis, George, Inspector, Cyprus Police Force, Nicosia, Cyprus.

Lambrou, Andreas, dentist and EOKA arms storeman, Nicosia, Cyprus.

Lennox-Boyd, Rt. Hon. Alan, Colonial Secretary, British Government, London, England.

Louka, Gregoris, bodyguard to Gen. Grivas, Nicosia, Cyprus.

Lyssarides, Vassos, personal physician to President Makarios, Nicosia, Cyprus.

Lyssiotis, Renos, attorney, EOKA youth leader, Nicosia, Cyprus.

Makarios III (Michael Mouskos), Archbishop and President of Cyprus.

Macmillan, Harold, Prime Minister of Gt. Britain, London, England.

Menderes, Adnan, Prime Minister of Turkey. Ankara, Turkey.

Markidou, Mrs. Maroulla, EOKA courier, youth leader, Nicosia, Cyprus.

Nikitas, Pavlos, member of mountain guerrilla band under Grivas, Nicosia, Cyprus.

Noel-Baker, Francis, Member of Parliament (Labour), London, England.

Panayides, Daphnis, aide and housekeeper to Gen. Grivas, Limassol, Cyprus.

Papandreou, Andreas, Minister of State, Greek Government, Athens, Greece.

Papandreou, George, Prime Minister of Greece. Athens, Greece.

Pavlakis, Pavlos, EOKA group commander, Famagusta city, Famagusta, Cyprus.

Rigas, Andreas, Inspector, Cyprus Police, Nicosia, Cyprus.

Rodosthenous, Lefkios, EOKA group commander, Limassol district, Limassol, Cyprus.

Rossides, Michael, EOKA group commander, Larnaca district, Larnaca, Cyprus.

Sampson, Nicos, EOKA group leader, Nicosia, Cyprus.

Sofocleus, Tassos, EOKA group commander, Kyrenia district, Kyrenia, Cyprus.

Stokkos, Pavlos, Sergeant, Cyprus Police Force, Nicosia, Cyprus.

Tryfonides, Christakis, EOKA group leader, Limassol, Cyprus.

Xenofontos, Haralambos, member of EOKA mountain guerrilla group, Nicosia, Cyprus.

Zorlu, Fatin Rustu, Foreign Minister of Turkey. Ankara, Turkey.

General Works

Alastos, Doros. *Cyprus Guerrilla: Grivas, Mararios and the British*. London: Heinemann, 1960.

Alastos, Doros. *Cyprus in History*. London: Zeno Publishers, 1955.

Arnold, Percy. *Cyprus Challenge*. London: Hogarth Press, 1956.

Balfour, Patrick (Lord Kinross). *The Orphaned Realm*. London: Percival Marshall, 1951.

Barker, Dudley. *Grivas: Portrait of a Terrorist*. London: The Cresset Press, 1959.

Bilge, A. Suat. *Le Conflit de Chypre et les Cypriotes Turcs*. Ankara: University of Ankara, 1961.

Byford-Jones, W. *Grivas and the Story of EOKA*. London: Robert Hale, 1959.

Churchill, Winston S. *The Second World War*, 6 Vols. New York: Houghton Mifflin, 1953.

Dobell, William M. *A Respite for Cyprus*. Toronto: Canadian Institute of International Affairs, 1965.

Durrell, Lawrence. *Bitter Lemons*. New York: Dutton, 1959.

Eden, Anthony (Earl of Avon). *Full Circle*. Boston: Houghton Mifflin, 1960.

Foley, Charles. *Island in Revolt*. London: Longmans, 1962.

————. *Legacy of Strife*. London: Penguin Books, 1964.

Foot, Hugh (Lord Caradon). *A Start in Freedom*. London: Hodder and Stoughton, 1964; New York: Harper and Row, 1964.

Foot, Michael. *Guilty Men, 1957*. London: Gollancz, 1957.

Grivas, General George. *Guerrilla Warfare and EOKA's Struggle*. London: Longmans, 1964.

————. *Memoirs*. Edited by Charles Foley. London: Longmans, 1964; New York: Praeger, 1965.

Gunnis, Rupert. *Historic Cyprus*. London: Methuen, 1947.

Hill, Sir George. *History of Cyprus*, 4 Vols. Cambridge: Cambridge University Press, 1940–1952.

Le Geyt, Captain P. *Makarios in Exile*. Nicosia, Cyprus: Anagennisis Press, 1961.

Lenczowski, George. *The Middle East in World Affairs*. Ithaca, N.Y.: Cornell University Press, 1952.

Luke, Sir Harry. *Cyprus: An Appreciation*. New York: Roy, 1957.

Macmillan, Harold. *Riding the Storm, 1956–1959*. New York: Harper and Row, 1971.

Meyer, A. J. and Vassiliou, Simos. *The Economy of Cyprus*. Cambridge, Mass.: Harvard University Press, 1962.

Moneypenny, W. F. and Buckle, G. E. *The Life of Benjamin Disraeli*. 2 Vols. New York: Macmillan, 7th ed. 1929.

Monroe, Elizabeth. *The Mediterranean in Politics*. Oxford: Oxford University Press, 1938.

————. *Britain's Moment in the Middle East, 1914–1956*. London: Chatto and Windus, 1963.

Papandreou, A. *Democracy at Gunpoint: the Greek Front*. New York: Doubleday & Co., 1970.

Stephens, Robert. *Cyprus: a Place of Arms*. London: Pall Mall Press, 1966.

Storrs, Sir Ronald. *Orientations*. London: Nicholson and Watson, 1949.

Toynbee, Arnold J. *The Western Question in Greece and Turkey*. London: Constable, 1922.

Woodhouse, C. M. *Apple of Discord*. London: Hutchinson, 1948.

Public Documents and Pamphlets

Allegations of Brutality in Cyprus. Foreword by the Governor of Cyprus, Field Marshal Sir John Harding. Nicosia: Cyprus Government, 1957.

Annual Reports of the Director of Prisons. Nicosia: Cyprus Government, 1954–1959.

The Church and Terrorism in Cyprus, a Record of the Complicity of the Greek-Orthodox Church of Cyprus in Political Violence. Nicosia: Cyprus Government, 1957.

Corruption of Youth in Support of Terrorism. Nicosia: Cyprus Government, 1957.

Cyprus: a Handbook on the Island's Past and Present. Nicosia: Greek Communal Chamber, 1964.

Cyprus: EOKA's Campaign of Terror. London: Central Office of Information, 1956.

The Cyprus Problem Before the United Nations. Nicosia: Public Information Office, 1966.

Cyprus: Touchstone of Democracy. Athens: Union of Journalists, 1958.

Economic Review, 1955–1956. Nicosia: Cyprus Government, 1957.

EOKA leaflets, 1955–1957. Nicosia: Public Information Office, 1957.

Greek Minority in Turkey and Turkish Minority in Greece. Athens: Greek Information Service, 1965.

Great Britain, *Parliamentary Debates,* (Common and Lords) 1954–1960.

Great Britain, *Parliamentary Papers,* "Constitutional Proposals for Cyprus," (Radcliffe Report), Cmd. 42, 1956.

Great Britain, *Parliamentary Papers,* "Correspondence between the Governor of Cyprus and Archbishop Makarios," Cmd. 9708, 1956.

Great Britain, *Parliamentary Papers,* "Cyprus" (The London and Zurich Agreements), Cmd. 1093, 1960.

Great Britain, *Parliamentary Paper,* (Commons), "Tripartite Conference on Cyprus," Cmd. 9594, 1955.

Royal Institute for International Affairs, *Cyprus: Background to Enosis.* (Oxford University Press, 1958.)

———— *Cyprus: the Dispute and the Settlement.* (Oxford University Press, 1959.)

Terrorism in Cyprus: The Captured Documents. London: HMSO, 1956.

The Turkish Case, 70–30, and the Greek Tactics. Nicosia: Turkish Communal Chamber, 1963.

Turkey and Cyprus: Official Statements of the Turkish Viewpoint. London: Turkish Embassy, 1956.

Two Years in Cyprus: public statements by Sir Hugh Foot, Governor of Cyprus. Nicosia: Cyprus Government, 1960.

Whither Cyprus? Commentaries from the Cyprus Broadcasting Service. Nicosia: Cyprus Government, 1957.

Other Sources

Other sources consulted include the *Annual Report: Cyprus* (Nicosia) for the years 1954–1958, and various newspapers and journals, especially *The Times* (London), *The Observer* (London), *The Daily Telegraph* (London), *The Guardian* (London), *The Times of Cyprus* (Nicosia), and *Cyprus Mail* (Nicosia).

Index

Acheson, Dean, 164, 167
Afxentiou, Gregoris, 36-37, 67, 83, 93, 96, 118-122
AKEL (Progressive Party of the Working People). *See* Communists, Cypriot
Aristotelous, Kyriakos, 51, 84
Armitage, Sir Robert, 42, 47
Athens Radio, 42, 53, 72, 76, 83
Averoff, Evangelos, 86, 149, 153-156, 161
Azinas, Andreas, 17, 22, 28, 31-32, 75, 114, 130-131, 152

Baker, Brigadier George, 87
Ball, George, 162
Bases, military, 156, 157
Bourke, Sir Paget, 141

Cannon, Cavendish, 99
Caraolis, Michael, 52-53, 85
Castle, Barbara, 144, 148
Chartas, Andreas, 67, 104, 117
Christodoulides, Marios and Elli, 108-110, 117, 128, 158
Civil war, of 1963, 162
Clerides, Glafkos, 134
Clerides, John, 124
Collective fines, 65
Communists, Cypriot, 9, 42, 53, 66
Counter-insurgency techniques. *See* Security Forces
Curfews, 65, 82, 128
Cyprus Broadcasting Service, 29, 41, 54, 129, 143
Cyprus Mail, 30, 42, 47, 65

Darling, General Kenneth, 150
Dear, William H., 133
Detention camps, British, 65, 133, 135

'Dighenis Akritas', 5, 40
Disraeli, Benjamin, 1
Drakos, Markos, 40, 47, 51, 67, 70, 83, 94, 111, 120
Droushiotis, Yannakis, 42
Dulles, John Foster, 50, 56

Eden, Sir Anthony, 9, 21, 43, 50, 56, 76-77, 79, 89-90, 98, 100, 102, 126
Eisenhower, Dwight D., 72, 76-77
Eliades, Socrates, 130, 152, 155, 156
Emergency Regulations, 64
EOKA (National Organization of Cypriot Fighters): arms smuggling techniques, 20-22, 28-34, 57-59, 75, 114, 131, 152, 153; execution squads, 98-99, 104-107, 147-148; diversionary tactics, 61, 88-89; routed in mountains, 118-125; survival of, 127-129, 132-133; suspends action, 126, 129; Turkish-Cypriots clash with, 141; captive leaders freed, 158; factional split, 161
Evangelakis, Evangelos, 37, 51

Foot, Sir Hugh (Lord Caradon), 129, 131-132, 134-135, 140, 148, 155-157, 159

Gabrielides, Gabriel, 127
Georgadjis, Polycarpos, 38, 45, 54, 103, 120, 137, 153, 160
Georghiades, Antonis, 89, 90-91, 109, 117, 135-137, 155, 158
Greece: British offer to cede Cyprus to, 3; quarrel with British over Cyprus, 15; urges cease-fire, 126; supports independent Cyprus, 144, 148; clash with Turkey, 165; Zurich-London agreement, 156;